THE LORD'S SUPPER

CW00550486

THE LORD'S SUPPER

Thomas Watson

'This is my body . . . this is my blood of the
new testament' (*Matt.* 26:26–28).

THE BANNER OF TRUTH TRUST

THE BANNER OF TRUTH TRUST
3 Murrayfield Road, Edinburgh EH12 6EL, UK
P.O. Box 621, Carlisle, PA 17013, USA

*

First published as *The Holy Eucharist*, 1665
First Banner of Truth edition, 2004
ISBN 0 85151 854 0

*

Typeset in 10¹/₂/14 pt Sabon at the
Banner of Truth Trust, Edinburgh
Printed and bound in the UK
by Bell & Bain Ltd.,
Glasgow.

*

*'Dedit nobis Christus carnem suam in cibum,
sanguinem in potum, animam in pretium,
aquam lateris in lavacrum'* –
Christ gave us his flesh for food, his blood
for drink, his soul as our price, the water
from his side for our cleansing
– *Bernard of Clairvaux*
(from the original
title-page).

Contents

Epistle to the Reader

CHRISTIAN READER,

When I contemplate the holiness and solemnity of the blessed sacrament, I cannot but have some ache upon my spirit, and think myself bound to hold this mystery in the highest veneration. The elements of bread and wine are in themselves common but, under these symbolical representations, lie hid divine excellencies. Behold here the best of dainties, God is in his cheer. Here is the apple of the Tree of Life; here is the 'banqueting house' where the banner of free grace is gloriously displayed, 'He brought me to the banqueting house, and his banner over me was love' (*Song of Sol.* 2:4).

In the sacrament we see Christ broken before us, and his broken body is the only comfort for a broken heart. While we sit at this table, Christ's precious spikenard of merit and grace sends forth its fragrance. The sacrament is both a healing and a sealing ordinance. Here our Saviour leads his people up the Mount of Transfiguration, and gives them a glimpse of paradise. How

[vii]

welcome should this jubilee of the soul be, wherein Christ appears in the splendour of his beauty, and draws the golden lines of love to the centre of a believer's heart.

Oh! What flames of devotion should burn in our hearts! How agile and nimble should we be, mounting up as on wings of cherubim, when we are able to meet the Prince of Glory, who brings the olive-branch of peace in his mouth, and whose kisses leave a print of heaven upon the soul. The scope of this ensuing discourse is to excite holy ardours of soul in such as intend to partake of it.

Think not that it is enough to be outwardly devout at God's table, drawing near to him with the lip, when the heart is far from him, 'Wherefore the Lord said, Forasmuch as this people draw near me with their mouth, and with their lips do honour me, but have removed their heart far from me, and their fear toward me is taught by the precept of men: therefore, behold, I will proceed to do a marvellous work among this people, even a marvellous work and a wonder: for the wisdom of their wise men shall perish, and the understanding of their prudent men shall be hid' (*Isa.* 29:13–14). What is this but, with Ephraim, to compass God with lies (*Hos.* 11:12)? They who put off God with bare shows, he will put them off with bare signs. They who give God only the skin of duty shall carry away only the shell of comfort.

Spirituality is the life of worship. If we come to the sacrament in due order, we shall see him whom our souls love, 'But let a man examine himself, and so let him eat of that bread, and drink of that cup' (*1 Cor.* 11: 28).

The Lord will give us a foretaste here, and reserve the after-taste of glory for the kingdom of heaven. That this may be effected shall be the earnest prayer of him who is,

Yours in the work of the gospel,
THOMAS WATSON
London, 1665.

Publisher's Foreword

This rare work was originally published in 1665 with the title *The Holy Eucharist, or the Mystery of the Lord's Supper Briefly Explained*. Though brief, it is worthy to rank alongside the other writings of Thomas Watson republished by the Trust.[1]

To Watson, the Lord's Supper was a mirror in which to behold the sufferings and death of Christ, and was, in certain respects, a more excellent means of grace than the preaching of the Word: 'A sacrament is a visible sermon. And herein the sacrament excels the Word preached. The Word is a trumpet to proclaim Christ, the sacrament is a glass to represent him . . . The Lord condescends to our weakness . . . God, to help our faith, does not only give us an audible Word, but a visible sign.'

[1] *A Body of Divinity, The Ten Commandments,* and *The Lord's Prayer,* which together make up Watson's *Body of Practical Divinity,* and, in the Puritan Paperbacks series, *All Things for Good, The Doctrine of Repentance,* and *The Godly Man's Picture.*

He believed that the sacrament was a priceless gift of the Saviour to the church, in the right use of which the faith of the people of God would be confirmed and strengthened, and their souls receive great benefit.

Two extremes, he believed, were to be avoided. One was the doctrine of transubstantiation, which was contrary both to Scripture and to reason and profaned Christ's institution of the Supper. The other was the error of those who looked on the Supper as only an empty shadow with no intrinsic efficacy to believers: 'Why is the Lord's Supper called "the communion of the body of Christ" (*1 Cor.* 10:16), but because, in the right celebration of it, we have sweet communion with Christ? . . . Such as make the sacrament only a representation of Christ do aim short of the mystery, and come short of the comfort.' This view builds on the teaching of Calvin who considered the sacrament a means of grace by which, through faith, Christ worked effectually in the believer.

Some Protestants have been disposed to dissent from this position, but none who love our Lord Jesus Christ will fail to be moved and blessed by the warmth and devotion to the Saviour found in Watson's exposition.

The publishers wish to thank Mr Roger N. McDermott who carefully transcribed Watson's work from a copy in the Bodleian Library, Oxford, and helped to prepare it for publication.

THE PUBLISHER
Edinburgh
January 2004

I

The Mystery of the Lord's Supper

*And as they were eating, Jesus took bread, and blessed it,
and brake it, and gave it to the disciples, and said, Take,
eat; this is my body. And he took the cup, and gave thanks,
and gave it to them, saying, Drink ye all of it; for this
is my blood of the new testament, which is shed for
many for the remission of sins* (Matt. 26:26–28).

In these words, we have the institution of the Lord's
Supper. The Greeks call the sacrament *musterion*: a
mystery. There is in it a mystery of wonder, and a mystery
of mercy. 'The celebration of the Lord's Supper is the
commemoration of the greatest blessing that ever the
world enjoyed', says Chrysostom.[1] A sacrament is a

---

[1] John Chrysostom (347–407), the 'golden-mouthed'; bishop of
Constantinople and an outstanding preacher.

visible sermon. And herein the sacrament excels the Word preached. The Word is a trumpet to proclaim Christ, the sacrament is a glass to represent him.

QUESTION: But why was the sacrament of the Lord's Supper appointed? Is not the Word sufficient to bring us to heaven?

ANSWER: The Word is for the engrafting, the sacrament for the confirming of faith. The Word brings us to Christ, the sacrament builds us up in him. The Word is the font where we are baptized with the Holy Spirit, the sacrament is the table where we are fed and cherished. The Lord condescends to our weakness. Were we made up all of spirit, there would be no need of bread and wine, but we are compounded creatures. Therefore God, to help our faith, does not only give us an audible Word, but a visible sign. *'Et sensus fovetur, et fides firmatur'* [Sense is fed, and faith is strengthened]. I may here allude to that of our Saviour, Except ye see signs . . . ye will not believe (*John* 4:48). 'Because we are led by external things, God increases faith in us by these symbols' (Gualter).[1]

Things taken in by the eye do work upon us more than things taken in by the ear. A solemn spectacle of mortality does more affect us than an oration. So when we see Christ broken in the bread, and as it were crucified before us, this does more affect our hearts than the bare preaching of the cross.

---

[1] *Quia externis ducimur, hisce symbolis fidem in nobis adauget Deus.* Rudolf Gualter (1519–86) was a Swiss Reformer and Bullinger's successor in Zurich.

So I come to the text in Matthew 26:26–28, where I shall open, in the first three chapters, these five particulars in reference to the sacrament:

1. *the Author,* 2. *the Time,* 3. *the Manner,* 4. *the Guests,* and 5. *the Benefits.*

1. *The Author of the Sacrament Is Jesus Christ.*

'Jesus took bread.' To institute sacraments belongs of right to Christ, and is a flower of his crown. He only who can give grace can appoint the sacraments, which are the seals of grace. Christ being the founder of the sacrament gives a glory and a lustre to it. A king making a feast adds all the more state and magnificence to it. 'Jesus took bread', he whose Name is above every name (*Phil.* 2:9); God blessed for ever.

2. *The Time When Christ Instituted the Sacrament.*

As to the time when Christ did institute the sacrament, we may take notice of two circumstances.

i. It was when he had supped (*Luke* 22:20: 'after supper'); which had this mystery in it, to show that the Sacrament is chiefly intended as a *spiritual* banquet; it is not to indulge the senses but to feed the graces. It was '*after* supper'.

ii. The other circumstance of time is that Christ did appoint the sacrament a little before his sufferings. 'The Lord Jesus the same night in which he was betrayed took bread' (*1 Cor.* 11:23). He knew troubles were now coming upon his disciples; it would be no small perplexity to them to see their Lord and Master crucified; and shortly after they must pledge him a bitter cup; therefore, to arm them against such a time, and to animate their spirits, that very night in which he was betrayed he gives them his body and blood in the sacrament.

This may give us a good hint, that, in all trouble of mind, especially in approaches of danger, it is needful to have recourse to the Lord's Supper. The sacrament is both an antidote against fear and a restorative to faith. 'The night in which he was betrayed, he took bread' (*1 Cor.* 11:23).

3. *The Manner of the Institution*, wherein there are four things observable:

i.   The taking of bread
ii. The blessing of it
iii. The breaking of it
iv. The administering of the cup.

i. *The taking of bread*, 'Jesus took bread.'

QUESTION: What is meant by this phrase, 'He took bread'?

ANSWER: Christ's taking the bread from common uses did hold forth a double mystery.

a. It signified that God in his eternal decree set Christ apart for the work of our redemption. He was *kechorismenos*, separate from sinners (*Heb.* 7:26).

b. Christ's setting the elements apart from common bread and wine showed that he is not for common persons to feed on. They are to be divinely purified who touch these holy things of God. They must be outwardly separated from the world, and inwardly sanctified by the Spirit.

QUESTION: Why did Christ take bread, rather than any other element?

ANSWER: Because it did *prefigure* Him. Christ was typified (a) *by the shewbread*: 'And Solomon made all the vessels that pertained unto the house of the LORD: the altar of gold, and the table of gold, whereupon the shewbread was' (*1 Kings* 7:48); (b) *by the bread which Melchizedek offered unto Abraham*. 'And Melchizedek king of Salem brought forth bread and wine' (*Gen.* 14:18); and (c) *by the cake which the Angel brought to Elijah*. 'And he looked, and, behold, there was a cake baken on the coals' (*1 Kings* 19:6). Therefore Christ took the bread to answer the type.

Christ took bread also because of the *analogy*; bread did nearly resemble him: 'I am that bread of life' (*John* 6:48). There is a threefold resemblance.

a. *Bread is useful.* Other comforts are more for delight than use. Music delights the ear, colours the eye, but bread is the staff of life. So is Christ useful. There is no subsisting without him, 'He that eateth me, even he shall live by me' (*John* 6:57).

b. *Bread is satisfying*. If a man be hungry and you bring him flowers or pictures, they do not satisfy, but bread does fully satisfy. So Jesus Christ, the bread of the soul, satisfies; he satisfies the eye with beauty, the heart with sweetness, the conscience with peace.

c. *Bread is strengthening*. 'Bread which strengtheneth man's heart' (*Psa.* 104:15). So Christ, the bread of the soul, transmits strength. He strengthens us against temptations, he gives strength for doing and suffering work. He is like the cake the Angel brought to the prophet, 'He arose, and did eat and drink, and went in the strength of that meat, forty days and forty nights unto Horeb the Mount of God' (*1 Kings* 19:8).

ii. The second thing in the institution is *Christ's blessing of the bread*. He blessed it: 'By the blessing of Christ, common bread was changed into a holy use' (Gualter).[1] This was the consecration of the elements. Christ, by his blessing, sanctified them, and made them symbols of his body and blood: '*Consecration* is a pious term signifying that by which things foreign to religious mysteries may be the sacrament of the body and blood of Christ' (Chamier, *De Eucharistia*).[2] Our consideration of this is continued in the next chapter.

[1] *Benedictione Christi panis communis in sacrum mutatus est.*

[2] *Consecratio vocabulum est solenne significans id quo per se aliena sunt a mysteriis religiosis, sint sacramenta corporis et sanguinis Christi.* The reference is to a work by Daniel Chamier published in Geneva in 1626.

2

The Consecration of
the Elements

Jesus took bread, and blessed it . . . and he took the cup, and gave thanks (Matt. 26:26–27).

Three things may be seen in Christ's consecrating the elements.

a. *Christ, in blessing the elements opened the nature of the sacrament to the Apostles*. In so doing, he solved this mystery. Christ revealed to them that, as surely as they did receive the elements *corporeally*, so surely did they receive him into their hearts, *spiritually*.

b. *Christ's blessing the elements signified his prayer for a blessing upon the ordinance*. He prayed that these symbols of bread and wine might, through the blessing and operation of the Holy Spirit, sanctify the elect, and seal up all spiritual mercies and privileges to them.

c. *Christ's blessing the elements was his giving thanks.*
'[Giving thanks] was always the custom of the Jews, as
appears from the Talmudic writers, before taking food or
wine' (Josephus).[1] So it is in the Greek: *Eucharistia*; 'He
gave thanks.'

Christ gave thanks that God the Father had, in the
infinite riches of his grace, given his Son to expiate the
sins of the world. And if Christ gave thanks, how may we
give thanks! If he gave thanks, who was to shed his blood,
how may we give thanks, who are to drink it!

Christ gave thanks that God had given these elements
of bread and wine, not only to be signs but seals of our
redemption. As the seal serves to make over a convey-
ance of land, so the sacrament as a spiritual seal, serves
to make over Christ and heaven, to such as worthily
receive it.

iii. The third thing in the institution is *the breaking of
bread.* 'He brake it.' This did foreshadow Christ's death
and passion, with all the torments of his body and soul:
'It pleased the LORD to bruise him' (*Isa.* 53:10). When
spices are bruised, then they send forth a sweet savour. So
when Christ was bruised on the cross, he did send out a
most fragrant smell. Christ's body being crucified was the
breaking open of a box of precious ointment, which did
fill heaven and earth with its perfume.

[1] *Moris semper iudaeis fuit, ut ex thalmudicis scriptoribus
apparet, ante cibum aut vinum sumptum.* Josephus was a Jewish
historian, 37–100 AD.

QUESTION: But why was Christ's body broken? What was the cause of his suffering?

ANSWER: Surely not for any desert of his own: 'Messiah shall be cut off, but not for himself' (*Dan.* 9:26). In the original Hebrew it is, 'He shall be cut off, and there is nothing in him.' There is no cause in him why he should suffer. The High Priest, when he went into the tabernacle, offered first 'for himself' (*Heb.* 9:7); though he had his mitre, and golden plate, and wore holy garments, yet he was not pure and innocent; he must offer sacrifice for himself, as well as for the people. But Jesus Christ, that great High Priest, though he offered a bloody sacrifice, yet *not for himself*.

QUESTION: Why then was his blessed body broken?

ANSWER: It was for our sins. 'Thou grievest, Lord, not over thy wounds but over mine' (Ambrose).[1] 'But he was wounded for our transgressions' (*Isa.* 53:5). The Hebrew word for wounded has a double emphasis; either it may signify that he was pierced through as with a dart: *perforatus*; or that he was profaned: *profanatus*. He was used as some common vile thing; and Christ might thank us for it, 'He was wounded for our transgressions.' 'One sins and another is punished' (Luther).[2] So that if the question were put to us, as once to Christ, 'Prophesy, who

---

[1] *Doles, Domine, non tua vulnera sed mea.* Ambrose (340–97), Latin father known for his unflinching character and preaching ability.

[2] *Alius peccat, alius plectitur.*

is it that smote thee?' (*Luke* 22:64), we might soon answer, It was our sins that smote him. Our pride made Christ wear a crown of thorns. As Zipporah said to Moses, 'A bloody husband art thou to me' (*Exod.* 4:25); so may Christ say to his church, A bloody spouse thou hast been to me; thou has cost me my heart-blood.

QUESTION: But how could Christ suffer, being God? The Godhead is impassible.

ANSWER: Christ suffered only in his human nature, not the divine. Damascene[1] explains it by this simile: if one pour out water on iron that is red hot, the fire suffers by the water, and is extinguished, but the iron does not suffer. So the human nature of Christ might suffer death, but the divine nature is not capable of any passion. When Christ was, in the human nature, suffering, he was, in the divine nature, triumphing. As we wonder at the rising of the Sun of Righteousness in his incarnation, so we may wonder at the going down of this Sun in his passion.

QUESTION: But if Christ suffered only in his human nature, how could his suffering satisfy for sin?

ANSWER: By reason of the hypostatical[2] union, the human nature being united to the divine; the human nature did suffer, the divine did satisfy. Christ's Godhead did give both majesty and efficacy to his sufferings. Christ

[1] John of Damascus (Damascenus), ?676–760.
[2] A term used to denote the union between the divine and human natures in Christ.

was Sacrifice, Priest and Altar. He was sacrifice as he was man, Priest as he was God and man, Altar as he was God. It is the property of the altar to sanctify the thing offered on it (*Matt.* 23:14).

So the altar of Christ's divine nature sanctified the sacrifice of his death, and made it meritorious.

Now concerning Christ's suffering upon the cross, observe two things.

1. *The bitterness of it to him:* 'He was broken'. The very thoughts of his suffering put him into an agony. 'And being in an agony he prayed more earnestly: and his sweat was as it were great drops of blood falling down to the ground' (*Luke* 22:44)

He was as full of sorrow, as his heart could hold, 'My soul is exceeding sorrowful, even unto death' (*Matt.* 26:38).

Christ's crucifixion was (i) *a lingering death*. It was more for Christ to suffer one hour than for us to have suffered forever; but his death was lengthened out, he hung three hours upon the cross. He died many deaths before he could die one. 'Death involves less pain than waiting for death' (Ovid).[1]

(ii) *It was a painful death*. His hands and feet were nailed, which parts being full of sinews, and therefore very tender, his pain must needs be most acute and sharp; and to have the venomous arrow of God's wrath shot to

[1] *Morsque minus poenae, quam mora mortis habet* (Ovid, *Ep. Heroides*, x.82).

his heart, this was the direful catastrophe, and caused that vociferation and outcry upon the cross: 'My God, my God, why hast thou forsaken me?' (*Matt.* 27:46; *Mark* 15:34). The justice of God was now inflamed, and heightened to its fullest extent. God 'spared not his own Son' (*Rom.* 8:32). Nothing must be abated of the debt. Christ felt the pains of hell, though not locally, yet equivalently. In the sacrament we see this tragedy acted before us.

(iii) *It was a shameful death.* Christ is *in medio positus*, placed in the midst; he hung between two thieves (*Matt.* 27:38), as if he had been the principal malefactor. Well might the lamp of heaven withdraw its light, and mask itself in darkness, as if blushing to behold the Sun of Righteousness in an eclipse. It is hard to say which was greater, the blood of the cross or the shame of the cross (*Heb.* 12:2).

(iv) *It was a cursed death* (*Deut.* 21:23). This kind of death was so execrable that Constantine made a law that no Christian should die upon the cross. The Lord Jesus Christ underwent this: 'Being made a curse for us' (*Gal.* 3:13). He who was 'God blessed forever' (*Rom.* 9:5) was under a curse.

2. *Consider the sweetness of it to us*: 'No sooner was it done than it was beneficial.' Christ's bruising is our healing: 'With his stripes we are healed' (*Isa.* 53:5). Calvin calls the crucifixion of Christ, *Cardo salutis*, the hinge on

---

[1] *Non citius fuit, quam profuit.*

which our salvation turns: and Luther calls it *Fons salutis*, a gospel-spring, opened to refresh sinners. Indeed the suffering of Christ is a death-bed cordial; it is an antidote to expel our fear.

Does sin trouble? Christ has overcome it for us. Besides the two thieves crucified with Christ, there were two other invisible thieves crucified with him: sin and the devil.

iv. The fourth particular in the institution of the Lord's Supper is *Christ's administering the cup*: 'And he took the cup.' The taking of the cup showed the redundancy[1] of merit in Christ, and the copiousness of our redemption. Christ was not sparing, he gave not only bread, but the cup. We may say as the Psalmist, 'With the LORD . . . is plenteous redemption' (*Psa.* 130:7).

If Christ gave the cup, how dare the Papists withhold it? They clip and mutilate the ordinance. They blot out Scripture, and may fear that doom, 'If any man shall take away from the words of the book of this prophecy, God shall take away his part out of the book of life' (*Rev.* 22:19).

QUESTION: What is meant by Christ's taking the cup?
ANSWER: The cup is figurative; it is a metonymy of the subject, the cup is put for the wine in it. By this, Christ signified the shedding of his blood upon the cross; when his blood was poured out, now the vine was cut, and did bleed; now was the 'Lily of the Valleys' dyed a purple

---

[1] That is, superabundance, overflowing.

colour. 'They gave him a scarlet robe, although he himself empurpled the vesture of his body much more nobly by the shedding of his blood' (Bernard).[1] But to us it is a cup of salvation. When Christ drank this cup of blood, we may truly say, he drank health to the world. It was 'precious blood' (*1 Pet.* 1:19). In this blood we see sin fully punished, and fully pardoned. Well may the spouse give Christ of her 'spiced wine', and the 'juice of her pomegranate' (*Song of Sol.* 8:2), when Christ has given her a draught of his warm blood, spiced with his love, and perfumed with the divine nature.

4. *The Guests Invited to the Lord's Supper*

The fourth thing is the guests invited to this Supper, or the persons to whom Christ distributed the elements; 'He gave it to the *disciples*, and said, Take, eat.' The sacrament is children's bread. If a man makes a feast, he calls his friends. Christ calls his disciples; if he had any piece better than another, he carves it to them.

'There is no room for more shades' (Horace).[2]

'This is my body which is given for you' (*Luke* 22:19). That is, for you 'pistoi', believers. Christ gave his body and blood to the disciples chiefly under this notion, as

---

[1] *Stolam coccineam dederunt ei, quamvis ipse vestem corporis sanguinaria effusione multo nobilius purpuravit.* Bernard of Clairvaux (1090–1153), called by Luther the most God-fearing monk of the Middle Ages.

[2] *Non locus est pluribus umbris.* In this context, a 'shade' was a guest not invited by the host but brought by some other guest of importance as one of his party.

they were believers. As Christ poured out his prayers (*John* 17), so his blood, only for believers; see how near to Christ's heart all believers lie! Christ's body was broken on the cross, and his blood shed for them. 'The election hath obtained it' (*Rom.* 11:7). Christ has passed by others, and died intentionally for them.

Impenitent sinners have no benefit by Christ's death, unless a short reprieve. Christ is given to the wicked in wrath. He is 'a rock of offence' (*1 Pet.* 2:8). The blood of Christ is like chemical drops of oil, which recover some patients, but kill others. Judas sucked death from the Tree of Life. God can turn stones into bread, and a sinner can turn bread into stones; the bread of life into the stone of stumbling.

3

The Benefits of the
Lord's Supper

My blood . . . is shed . . . or the remission of sins
(Matt. 26:28).

The fifth thing observable in the text (*Matt.* 26:26–28), is the benefit of this Supper, in these words: 'For the remission of sins'. This is a mercy of the first magnitude, the *summum genus*, the crowning blessing: 'Who forgiveth all thine iniquities . . . who crowneth thee with lovingkindness' (*Psa.* 103:3–4).

Whosoever has this charter granted is enrolled in the Book of Life: 'Blessed is he whose transgression is forgiven' (*Psa.* 32:1). Under the words 'remission of sins' by a synecdoche are comprehended all heavenly benedictions: justification, adoption, glory, in respect of which benefits we may, with Chrysostom, call the Lord's Supper 'the feast of the cross'.

This doctrine of the sacrament *confutes the opinion of transubstantiation*. 'It is not transubstantiation which is understood, nor transformation, but the sacramental uniting of the sign and the substance' (Beza).[1] When Christ says, 'This is my body', the Papists affirm that the bread, after consecration, is turned into the substance of Christ's body. We hold that Christ's body is in the sacrament spiritually, but the Papists say that it is there carnally; which opinion is both absurd and impious.

1. *It is absurd*, for it is contrary (i) *to Scripture*. The Scriptures assert that Christ's body is locally and numerically in heaven. 'Whom the heaven must receive until the times of restitution of all things' (*Acts* 3:21). If Christ's body be circumscribed in heaven, then it cannot be materially in the Lord's Supper.

It is contrary (ii) *to reason*. How is it imaginable that a thing should be changed into another species, yet continue the same? That the bread in the sacrament should be transmitted and turned into flesh, yet remain bread still? When the rod of Moses was turned into a serpent, it could not be at the same time both a rod and a serpent. That the bread in the sacrament should be changed into the body of Christ, and yet remain bread, is a perfect contradiction. If the Papists say the bread is vanished, this is fitter to be put into legend than our creed; for the colour, form and taste of the bread still remain.

---

[1] *Non Transubstantiatio intelligitur, vel transfusio, sed signi rei coniunctio sacramentalis* (Beza).

2. *This opinion of transubstantiation is impious*; as appears in two things:

i. *It is a profaning of Christ's body;* for if the bread in the sacrament be the real body of Christ, then it may be eaten not only by the wicked but by reptiles and vermin, which were to disparage and cast contempt upon Christ and his ordinance.

ii. *It runs men inevitably upon sin;* for through this mistake, that the bread is the very body of Christ, there follows the divine worship given to the bread, which is idolatry; as also the offering up of the bread, or host, in the Mass, which is a blasphemy against the priestly office of Christ, as if his sacrifice on the cross was imperfect.

Therefore I conclude with Peter Martyr[1] that this doctrine of transubstantiation is to be abhorred and exploded, being minted only by men's fancies, but not sprung up in the field of the Holy Scriptures.

This doctrine of the sacrament *confutes such as look upon the Lord's Supper only as an empty figure or shadow,* resembling Christ's death, but having no intrinsic efficacy in it. Surely this glorious ordinance is more than an effigy or representation of Christ. Why is the Lord's Supper called 'the communion of the body of Christ' (*1 Cor.* 10: 16), but because, in the right celebration

[1] Pietro Martire Vermigli (1499–1562), a leading Italian Reformer.

[18]

of it, we have sweet communion with Christ? In this gospel ordinance, Christ does not only show forth his beauty, but sends forth his virtue. The sacrament is not only a picture drawn, but a breast drawn; it gives us a taste of Christ, as well as a sight (*1 Pet.* 2:3). Such as make the sacrament only a representation of Christ do aim short of the mystery, and come short of the comfort.

The sacrament informs us of several things. It shows us the *necessity of coming to the Lord's Supper*. Has Jesus Christ gone to all this cost to make a feast? Then surely there must be guests. 'This do in remembrance of me' (*Luke* 22:19).

It is not left to our choice whether we will come or not, but it is a duty purely indispensable: 'Let him eat of that bread and drink of that cup' (*1 Cor.* 11:28). These words are not only permissive, but authoritative: as if a king should say, 'Let it be enacted.' The neglect of the sacrament runs men into a Gospel *Praemunire*.[1]

It was infinite goodness in Christ, to broach that blessed vessel of his body, and let his sacred blood stream out; and for us wilfully to omit such an ordinance, wherein the trophy of mercy is so richly displayed, and our salvation so nearly concerned – well may Christ take this as an undervaluing of him, and interpret it as no better than a bidding him keep his feast to himself.

---

[1] A writ summoning a person accused of suing in a foreign court for matters which could be tried by the law of England, used against papal claims. Watson implies that deliberate absence from the Lord's Supper is treason on the part of the believer.

He that observed not the passover, 'the same soul shall be cut off from among his people' (*Num.* 9:13). How angry was Christ with those that stayed away from the supper in the parable! They thought to put it off with a compliment, but Christ knew how to construe their excuse for a refusal: 'None of those men which were bidden shall taste of my supper' (*Luke* 14:24).

The rejecting of gospel-mercy is a sin of so deep a dye that God can do no less than punish it for a contempt. Some need a flaming sword to keep them off the Lord's table; and others need Christ's 'whip of small cords' to drive them to it.

Perhaps some will say they are above the sacrament. It is strange to hear a man say he is above his food! The apostles were not above this ordinance, and does anyone presume to be a peg higher than the apostles? Let all the enthusiasts consult that Scripture: 'As often as ye eat this bread, and drink this cup, ye do show the Lord's death till he come' (*1 Cor.* 11:26). The Lord's death is to be remembered sacramentally, till he come to judgment.

See the misery of unbelievers: though the Lord has appointed this glorious ordinance of his body and blood, they reap no benefit by it. They come indeed to the sacrament, either to keep up their credit, or to stop the mouth of conscience, but they get nothing for their souls. They come empty of grace, and go away empty of comfort: 'It shall even be as when an hungry man dreameth, and behold he eateth, but he awaketh, and his soul is empty' (*Isa.* 29:8). So wicked men fancy they eat of the spiritual banquet, but they are in a golden dream: 'Nothing remains to the wicked but an empty show' (Davenant).[1]

Alas, they fail to 'discern the Lord's body'. The manna lay round about Israel's camp, and they knew it not: 'They wist not what it was' (*Exod.* 16:15). So carnal persons see the external elements, but Christ is not known to them in his saving virtues: there is honey in the Spiritual Rock, which they never taste. They feed on the bread, but not Christ in the bread: 'They eat the bread of the Lord, but not the Bread which *is* the Lord.' Isaac ate the kid, when he thought it had been venison (*Gen.* 27:25). Unbelievers go away with the shadow of the sacrament; they have the rind and the husk, not the marrow. They eat the kid, not the venison.

---

[1] *Impiis nihil restat praeter inane spectaculum.* The quotation seems to be from Dr John Davenant, 1572–1641, Bishop of Salisbury.

[2] *Edunt panem Domini, non panem Dominum.*

4

Christ's Love Displayed
in the Sacrament

This is my blood of the new testament,
which is shed for many (Matt. 26:28).

S ee in this text, as in a glass, infinite love displayed.
1. *Behold the love of God the Father* in giving
Christ to be broken for us. That God should lay such a
jewel to pawn is the wonderment of angels: 'God so
loved the world, that he gave his only begotten Son'
(*John* 3:16). It is a pattern of love without parallel; it
was a far greater expression of love in God to give his
Son to die for us than if he had voluntarily acquitted us
of the debt, without any satisfaction at all. If a subject be
disloyal to his sovereign, it argues more love in the king
to give his own son to die for that subject than to forgive
him the wrong freely.

2. *Behold the amazing love of Christ.* His body was broken. The cross, says St Augustine, was a pulpit in which Christ preached his love to the world. Let us see in the cross, a holy culmination of the love of Christ.

i. *It was wonderful love that Christ who never had the viper of sin fastened on him should be reputed a sinner:* that he who hated sin, should be 'made sin' (*2 Cor.* 5:2l); that he who is numbered among the Persons of the Trinity should be 'numbered with the transgressors' (*Isa.* 53:12).

ii. *It was wonderful love that Christ should suffer death.* 'Lord,' says Bernard, 'thou hast loved me more than thyself, for thou didst lay down thy life for me.'[1] The Emperor Trajan[2] rent off a piece of his own robe, to bind up one of his soldier's wounds. Christ rent off his own flesh for us; nay, that Christ should die as the 'greatest sinner' (Luther), having the weight of all men's sins laid upon him, here was love *usque ad stuporem dulcis* (sweet to the point of astonishment). It sets all the angels in heaven wondering.

iii. *It was wonderful love that Christ should die freely:* 'I lay down my life' (*John* 10: 17); '[His acts] were not by

---

[1] *Dilexisti me, Domine, magis quam teipsum.*
[2] Trajan, Roman Emperor, 98–117 AD.

necessity, but by choice' (Jerome).[1] There was no law to enjoin him, no force to compel him. It is called the 'offering of the body of Jesus Christ' (*Heb.* 10:10). What could fasten him to the cross but the golden link of love?

iv. *It was wonderful love that Christ should die for such as we are.* What are we? Not only vanity, but enmity. When we were fighting, he was dying; when we had the weapons in our hands, then he had the spear in his side (*Rom.* 5:8).

v. *It was wonderful love that Christ died for us, when he could not expect to be at all bettered by us.* We were reduced to penury; we were in such a condition, that we could neither merit Christ's love nor requite it; for Christ to die for us, when we were at such a low ebb, was the very quintessence of love.

One man will extend kindness to another, so long as he is able to requite him; but if he be fallen to decay, then love begins to slacken and cool. But when we were engulfed in misery, and were fallen to decay, when we had lost our beauty, stained our blood, spent our portion, then Christ died for us. Oh, amazing love, which may swallow up all our thoughts!

vi. *It was wonderful love that Christ should not repent of his sufferings:* 'He shall see of the travail of his soul,

[3] *Non sunt ex necessitate, sed ex voluntate.* Jerome (340–420), biblical scholar and translator of the Latin Vulgate Bible.

and shall be satisfied' (*Isa.* 53:11). It is a metaphor that alludes to a mother who, though she has had hard labour, yet does not repent of it, when she sees a child born; so Christ had hard travail upon the cross, yet he does not repent of it, but thinks all his sweat and blood well bestowed, because he sees the man-child of redemption is brought forth into the world. 'He is fully contented with this one reward of his toil. Now he rests, now he has an abundance of delights.'[1] 'He shall be satisfied'; the Hebrew word signifies such a satiating as a man has at some sweet banquet.

vii. *It was wonderful love that Christ should rather die for us than for the angels that fell.* They were creatures of a more noble extract, and in all probability might have brought greater revenues of glory to God; yet that Christ should pass by those golden vessels, and make us clods of earth into stars of glory – Oh, the hyperbole of Christ's love!

viii. Yet another step of Christ's love (for, like the waters of the sanctuary, it rises higher): *It was wonderful love that Christ's love should not cease at the hour of death.* We write in our letters, 'Your friend until death!' But Christ wrote in another style, 'Your friend after death!' Christ died once, but loves ever. He is now testifying his affection to us; he is making the mansions ready for us,

---

[1] *Hoc uno laboris sui praemio affatim saturatur; nunc quiescit, nunc deliciis affluit.*

(*John* 14:2). He is interceding for us (*Heb.* 9:24). He appears in the court, as the Advocate for the client. When he has done dying, he has not done loving: 'They pierced with the inward spear of rage the side of Christ, which had been wounded long before with the spear of love' (Bernard).[1] Who can meditate upon this, and not be in an ecstasy? Well may the apostle call it, a love 'which passeth knowledge' (*Eph.* 3:14). When you see Christ broken in the sacrament, think of this love.

See then what dear and entire affections we should bear to Christ, who gives us his body and blood in the Eucharist. If he had had anything to part with of more worth, he would have bestowed it upon us. Oh, let Christ lie nearest our hearts. Let him be our Tree of Life, and let us desire no other fruit. Let him be our Morning Star, and let us rejoice in no other light.

As Christ's beauty, so his bounty should make him loved by us; he has given us his blood as the price, and his Spirit as the witness of our pardon. In the sacrament, Christ bestows all good things. He both imputes his righteousness, and imparts his loving-kindness. He gives a foretaste of that supper which shall be celebrated in the Paradise of God.

To sum up all, in the blessed Supper, Christ gives himself to believers; and what more can he give? Dear Saviour, how should thy Name be as 'ointment poured forth' (*Song of Sol.* 1:3)! The Persians worship the sun

---

[1] *Foderunt latus Christi intima furoris lancea, quod iam dudum amoris lancea fuit vulneratum.*

for their God, let us worship the Sun of Righteousness. Though Judas sold Christ for thirty pieces of silver, let us rather part with all than this Pearl. Christ is that Golden Pipe through which the golden oil of salvation is transmitted to us (see *Zech.* 4:12).

5

The Broken Body of Christ

This is my body
(Matt. 26:26).

The broken body of Christ exhibited to us in the sacrament should prompt us to reflect:

Was Christ's body broken?

Then we may behold sin odious in the red glass of Christ's sufferings. It is true, sin is to be abominated because it turned Adam out of Paradise, and threw the angels down to hell. Sin is the peace-breaker, it is like an incendiary in the family, that sets husband and wife at variance; it makes God fall out with us. Sin is the womb of our sorrows, and the grave of our comforts.

But that which may most of all disfigure the face of sin, and make it appear ghastly, is this, it crucified our Lord: it made Christ veil his glory and lose his blood.

If a woman saw that sword which killed her husband, how hateful would the sight of it be to her! Do we count that sin light, which made Christ's soul 'exceeding sorrowful unto death' (*Mark* 14:34)? Can that be our joy, which made the Lord Jesus Christ 'a man of sorrows' (*Isa.* 53:3)? Did he cry out, 'My God, my God, why hast thou forsaken me?' (*Matt.* 27:46)? And shall not those sins be forsaken by us, which made Christ himself forsaken? Oh, let us look upon sin with indignation.

When a temptation comes to sin, let us say as David, 'Is not this the blood of the men that went in jeopardy of their lives?' (*2 Sam.* 23:17). So, let us say, Is not this the sin that poured out Christ's blood? Let our hearts be enraged against sin. When the Senators of Rome showed the people Caesar's bloody robe, they were incensed against them who slew him. Sin has rent the white robe of Christ's flesh, and dyed it a crimson colour; let us seek to be avenged of our sins. Under the law, if an ox gored a man, so that he died, the ox was to be killed (*Exod.* 21:28). Sin has pierced and gored our Saviour: let it die the death. What a pity it is that that should live which would not suffer Christ to live!

Was Christ's body broken?

Let us make this use of his suffering on the cross, to learn not to wonder much if we meet with troubles in the world. Did Christ suffer, who 'knew no sin'? And do we think it strange to suffer, who know nothing but sin? Did Christ feel the anger of God? And is it much for us to feel the anger of men? Was the Head crowned with thorns, and would the members lie among roses? Must we have our bracelets and diamonds, when Christ had the spear and nails going to his heart? Truly such as are guilty may well expect the lash, when he who was innocent could not go free.

A further use of the doctrine of the sacrament is of *exhortation*. The branches of this will occupy us for most of what follows.

Was Christ's precious body broken for us? Let us then be affected with the great goodness of Christ.

Who can tread upon these hot coals, and his heart not burn? Who can not cry out, with Ignatius,[1] 'Christ, my love, is crucified!'? If a friend should die for us, would not our hearts be much affected by his kindness? That the God of heaven should die for us, how should this stupendous mercy have a melting influence upon us! The body of Christ broken, is enough to break the most flinty heart. At our Saviour's passion, the very stones did cleave asunder: 'The rocks rent' (*Matt.* 27:51). He that is not affected with this has a heart harder than the stones. If Saul was so affected with David's mercy in sparing his life (*1 Sam.* 24.16), how

---

[1] A second-century bishop of Antioch, martyred at Rome.

may we be affected with Christ's kindness, who to spare our life, lost his own! Let us pray, that as Christ was 'cruci-fixus', so he may be 'cordi-fixus' – as he was fastened to the cross, so may he be fastened to our hearts.

Is Jesus Christ spiritually exhibited to us in the sacrament? Let us then set a high value and estimate on him.

Let us prize Christ's body. Every crumb of this bread of life is precious: 'My flesh is meat indeed' (*John* 6:55). It is 'the excellent Bread which transcends substance', as Cyprian[1] calls it.

The manna was a lively type and emblem of Christ's body. Manna was sweet: 'the taste of it was like wafers made with honey' (*Exod.* 16:31). It was a delicious meal; therefore it was called 'angels' food' (*Psa.* 78:25), for its excellency. So Christ, the Sacramental Manna, is sweet to a believer's soul: 'His fruit was sweet to my taste' (*Song of Sol.* 2:3). Everything of Christ is sweet; his Name is sweet, his virtues sweet. This 'Manna' sweetens 'the waters of Marah'.

Nay, Christ's flesh excels manna:

i. *Manna was food, but not physic.* If an Israelite had been sick, manna could not have cured him; but this

---

[1] *Panis eximius et supersubstantialis.* Cyprian was a third-century church father and martyr, Bishop of Carthage 249–58.

blessed manna of Christ's body is not only for food, but for medicine. 'The body of Christ is medicine to the sick' (Bernard).[1]

Christ has 'healing in his wings' (*Mal.* 4:2). He heals the blind eye, the hard heart. Take this medicine near your heart and it will heal you of all spiritual distempers.

ii. *Manna was corruptible:* it ceased when Israel came to Canaan; but this blessed manna of Christ's body will never cease. The saints shall feed with infinite delight, and soul satisfaction, upon Christ for all eternity. The joys of heaven would cease, if this manna should cease.

The manna was put in a golden pot in the ark, to be preserved there: so the blessed manna of Christ's body, being put in the golden pot of the divine nature, is laid up in the ark of heaven for the saints to feast upon forever. Well, then, may we say of Christ's blessed body, 'It is meat indeed.'

'The field of Christ's body being dug upon the cross, we find the pearl of salvation there.'[2]

---

[1] *Corpus Christi aegris medicina.*
[2] *Fosso agro corporis Christi, margarita salutis invenitur.*

6

The Blood of Christ

*This is my blood of the new testament, which is
shed for many for the remission of sins*
(Matt. 26:28).

Let us prize Christ's blood in the sacrament. It is
'drink indeed' (*John* 6:55). 'The grape cluster of my
body was taken to the winepress of the cross for thy
salvation, and from it was pressed the new wine of
thy redemption' (Bernard).[1] Here is the *Nectar* and
Ambrosia[2] which God himself delights to taste of. This is
both a balsam and a perfume. That we may set a still
higher value upon the blood of Christ, I shall show you
seven rare supernatural virtues in it.

[1] *Ego botrus carnis pro salute tua portatus sum ad torcularem
crucis, inde eliquatum est mustum tuae redemptionis.*

[2] In Greek mythology, the foods of the gods.

1. *Christ's blood is a reconciling blood.*

'You, that were sometime alienated, and enemies in your mind, yet now hath he reconciled in the body of his flesh, through death' (*Col.* 1:21–22). No sooner was the message brought to King David, 'Uriah is dead' (*2 Sam.* 11:21), than the anger of David was removed. No sooner was the blood of Christ poured out, than God's anger was pacified. Christ's blood is 'the blood of atonement'.

Nay, it is not only a sacrifice, but a 'propitiation' (*1 John* 2:2), which denotes bringing us into favour with God. It is one thing for a traitor to be pardoned, and another thing to be brought into favour. Sin cut us off from God, Christ's blood cements us to God. If we had had as much grace as the angels, it could not have wrought our reconciliation. If we offered up millions of sacrifices, if we had wept rivers of tears, this could never have appeased an angry Deity; only the blood of Christ can ingratiate us into God's favour, and make him look upon us with a smiling aspect. When Christ died, the veil of the temple was rent; this was not without a mystery, to show that through Christ's blood, the veil of our sins is rent, which interposed between God and us.

2. *Christ's blood is a quickening blood.*

'Whoso . . . drinketh my blood, hath eternal life' (*John* 6:54); it both begets life, and prevents death, 'the life of the flesh is in the blood' (*Lev.* 17:11). Sure enough, the life of our soul is in the blood of Christ. When we contract deadness of heart, and are like wine that has lost its spirits, Christ's blood has an elevating power, it puts vivacity into us, making us quick and lively in our motions. 'They shall mount up with wings as eagles' (*Isa.* 40:31).

3. *Christ's blood is a cleansing blood.*

'How much more shall the blood of Christ . . . purge your conscience?' (*Heb.* 9:14). As the merit of the blood of Christ pacifies God, so the virtue of it purifies us. It is the King of Heaven's bath. It is *lavacrum animae* (the washing place of the soul), a laver to wash in. It washes a crimson sinner milk white: 'The blood of Jesus Christ his Son cleanseth us from all sin' (*1 John* 1:7). The Word of God is a looking glass, to show us our spots; and the blood of Christ is a fountain to wash them away (*Zech.* 13:1).

But this blood will not wash if it be mingled with anything. Water will not wash clean except it is mingled with soap or camphor, but if we go to mingle anything with Christ's blood, either the merits of saints, or the prayer of angels, it will not wash.

Let the blood of Christ be pure and unmixed, and there is no spot but it will wash it away. It purged out Noah's drunkenness and Lot's incest.

Indeed, there is one spot so black that Christ's blood does not wash it away, and that is the sin against the Holy Spirit; not that there is not enough virtue in Christ's blood to wash it away; but he who has sinned that sin will not be washed; he condemns Christ's blood and 'tramples it underfoot' (*Heb.* 10:29).

4. *Christ's blood is a softening blood.*

There is nothing so hard but it may be softened if it lie steeping in his blood; it will soften a stone. Water will soften the earth, though it will not soften a stone, but the blood of Christ mollifies a stone, it softens a heart of stone. It turns flint into a spring (*Psa.* 114:8). The heart which before was like a piece hewn out of a rock, being steeped in Christ's blood becomes soft, and the waters of repentance flow from it.

How was the jailor's heart dissolved and made tender when 'the blood of sprinkling' was upon it! 'Sirs, what must I do to be saved?' (*Acts* 16:30). His heart was now like melting wax. God might set what seal and impression he would upon it.

5. *Christ's blood is a cooling blood*:
i. *It cools the heat of sin.*

The heart naturally is full of distempered heat; it must needs be hot, being 'set on fire of hell'. It burns in lust and passion; the blood of Christ allays this heat, it quenches the inflammation of sin.

ii. *It cools the heat of conscience.*

In time of desertion, conscience burns with the heat of God's displeasure; now the blood of Christ, sprinkled upon the conscience, cools and pacifies it. And in this sense, Christ is compared to 'rivers of water' (*Isa.* 32:2). When the heart burns, and is in an agony, Christ's blood is like water to the fire: it has a cooling and quenching virtue in it.

6. *Christ's blood is a comforting blood.*

It is good against fainting fits. Christ's blood is better than wine; though wine cheers the heart of a man that is well, yet it will not cheer his heart when he has a fit of the stone,[1] or when the pangs of death are upon him; but Christ's blood will cheer the heart at such a time. It is best in affliction. It cures the trembling of the heart. A conscience sprinkled with the blood of Christ can, like the nightingale, sing with a thorn in its breast. The blood of Christ can make a prison become a palace. It turned the martyrs' flames into beds of roses: 'The martyrs are beaten, they rejoice; they die and behold they triumph. Why? Because, steeped in the blood of the cross, they do not fear death but hope for it.'[2]

Christ's blood gives comfort at the hour of death. As a holy man once said on his death-bed, when they brought him a cordial, 'No cordial like the blood of Christ.'

7. *Christ's blood is a heaven-procuring blood.*

'Through the side of Christ, he threw open to us the gateway to heaven' (Bernard).[3] Israel passed through the Red Sea to Canaan. So, through the Red Sea of Christ's blood, we enter into the heavenly Canaan. 'Having therefore . . . boldness to enter into the holiest by the blood of

---

[1] An episode of pain resulting from kidney or gall stones.

[2] *Feriuntur martyres, gaudent; moriuntur, et ecce triumphant; quare? quia, sanguine crucis perfusi, non mortem metuunt, sed sperant.*

[3] *Per latus Christi nobis patefecit in coelum introitum.*

Jesus' (*Heb.* 10:19). Our sins did shut heaven. Christ's blood is the key which opens the gate of paradise for us. 'We die through the tree of knowledge; we rise through the tree of the cross.'[1] Hence Theodoret[2] calls the cross the 'Tree of Salvation', because the blood which trickled down the cross distils salvation.

Well, then, may we prize the blood of Christ, and with St Paul, determine 'not to know anything . . . save Jesus Christ, and him crucified' (*1 Cor.* 2:2). Kings' crowns are only crosses, but the cross of Christ is the only crown.

---

[1] *Morimur per lignum scientiae, orimur per lignum crucis.*
[2] A fifth-century Bible commentator and ecclesiastical historian.

7

Self-Examination

*But let a man examine himself, and so let him
eat of that bread, and drink of that cup*
(1 Cor. 11:28).

D oes Christ offer his body and blood to us in the
Supper? Then with what solemn preparation should
we come to such an ordinance! It is not enough to do
what God has appointed, but *as* he appointed. 'Prepare
your hearts unto the LORD' (*1 Sam.* 7:3). The musician
first puts his instrument in tune before he plays. The heart
must first be prepared, and put in tune, before it goes to
meet with God in this solemn ordinance of the sacrament.
Take heed of rashness and irreverence. If we come not
preparedly, we do not drink, but spill Christ's blood,
'Whosoever shall eat this bread, and drink this cup of the
Lord, unworthily, shall be guilty of the body and blood of

the Lord' (*1 Cor.* 11:27). That is, says Theophilus,[1] he shall be judged a shedder of Christ's blood. We read of a wine-cup of fury in God's hand (*Jer.* 25:15). He that comes unpreparedly to the Lord's Supper turns the cup in the sacrament into 'a cup of fury'; 'He changes the cup of blood into the cup of wrath.'[2]

Oh, with what reverence and devotion should we address ourselves to these holy mysteries! The saints are called 'vessels . . . prepared' (*Rom.* 9:23). If ever these vessels should be prepared, it is when they are to hold the precious body and blood of Christ. The sinner that is damned is first prepared. Men do not go to hell without some kind of preparation. They are 'vessels . . . fitted for destruction' (*Rom.* 9:22). If those vessels are prepared which are filled with wrath, much more are those to be prepared who are to receive Christ in the sacrament. Let us dress ourselves by a Scripture-mirror, before we come to the Lord's table; and, with the Lamb's wife, make ourselves ready (*Rev.* 19:7).

QUESTION: How should we be rightly qualified and prepared for the Lord's Supper?

ANSWER: If we would come with prepared hearts, we must come:

1. *With self-examining hearts*, 'But let a man examine himself, and so let him eat of that bread' (*1 Cor.* 11:28).

---

[1] Late second-century bishop of Antioch.

[2] *Calicem sanguinis mutat in calicem furoris.*

It is not enough that others think we are fit to come, but we must examine ourselves. The Greek word to examine, *dokimazo*, is a metaphor taken from the goldsmith, who does curiously try his metals. So before we come to the Lord's table, we are to make a curious and critical trial of ourselves by the Word.

Self-examination, being a reflexive act, is difficult: 'We would rather excuse a vice than drive it out' (Seneca).[1] It is hard for a man to look inward, and see the face of his own soul. The eye can see everything but itself.

But this probatory work is necessary:

i. If we do not examine ourselves, we are at a loss about our spiritual estate; we know not whether we are interested in the covenant, or whether we have a right to the seal.

ii. God will examine us. It was a sad question the master of the feast asked, 'Friend, how camest thou in hither, not having a wedding garment?' (*Matt.* 22:12). So it will be terrible, when God shall say to a man, 'How camest thou in hither to my table with a proud, vain, unbelieving heart? What has thou to do here in thy sins? Thou pollutest my holy things.' What need therefore, is there to make a heart-search before we come to the Lord's Supper!

We would examine our sins, that they may be mortified; our wants, that they may be supplied; our graces, that they may be strengthened. 'He bids not one examine another, but a man himself, making the tribunal not a

[1] *Malumus vitium excusare quam excutere.*

public one, and the conviction without a witness'
(Chrysostom).

2. *We must come with serious hearts.* Our spirits are
feathery and light; like a vessel without ballast, which
floats upon the water, but does not sail. We float in holy
duties, and are full of vain excursions, even when we are
to deal with God, and are engaged in matters of life and
death. That which may consolidate our hearts, and make
them set with seriousness, is to consider that God's eye is
now especially upon us, when we approach to his table.
'The king came in to see the guests' (*Matt.* 22:11); God
knows every communicant, and if he sees any levity and
indecency of spirit in us unworthy of his presence, he will
be highly incensed, and send us away with the guilt of
Christ's blood, instead of the comfort of it.

3. *We must come with intelligent hearts.* There ought
to be a competent measure of knowledge, that we may
'discern the Lord's body'. As we are to 'pray with the
understanding' (*1 Cor.* 14:15), so ought we to communi-
cate at the Lord's table with understanding.

If knowledge be wanting, it cannot be a 'reasonable
service' (*Rom.* 12:1). They that know not the mystery, feel
not the comfort. We must know God the Father in his
attributes, God the Son in his offices, God the Holy Spirit
in his graces. Some say they have good hearts, yet lack
knowledge; we may as well call that a good eye which
lacks sight.

4. *We must come to the sacrament with longing hearts.*
We should say, as Christ, 'With desire I have desired to eat
this passover' (*Luke* 22:15). If God prepares a feast, we
must get an appetite. Why has the Lord frowned upon his
people of late but to punish their apathy, and provoke
their appetite? As David longed for the water of the well
of Bethlehem (*2 Sam.* 23:15), so should we long for Christ
in the sacrament. Desires are the sails of the soul, which
are spread to receive the gale of an heavenly blessing. To
help to excite holy desires and longings:

i. *Consider the magnificence and royalty of this Supper*:
it is a heavenly banquet. 'In this mountain shall the Lord
of hosts make unto all people a feast of fat things, a feast
of wines on the lees' (*Isa.* 25:6); 'These are the sweet
delights, here are drunk the rivers of honey, the draughts
of heavenly balm' (Bernard). Here is the juice of that
grape which comes from the true vine. Under these
elements of the bread and wine, Christ and all his benefits
are exhibited to us. The sacrament is *abunde aromatum*
(abundantly fragrant), a repository and storehouse of
celestial blessings. Behold here life, and peace, and
salvation are set before us! All the *dulcia fercula* [sweet
delicacies] of heaven are served at this feast.

ii. *To provoke appetite, consider what need we have of
this spiritual repast.* The angel persuaded Elijah to take a

---

[1] *Hae sunt suaves delitiae, hic bibuntur flumina mellis, liquores
balsami coelestis.*

little of the cake, and of the cruse of water, that he might not faint in his journey: 'Arise and eat, because the journey is too great for thee' (*1 Kings* 19:7). So, truly, we have a great journey from earth to heaven, therefore we have need to recruit ourselves by the way. How many sins have we to subdue! How many duties to perform! How many wants to supply! How many graces to strengthen! How many adversaries to conflict with! So that we do not abate by the way, by feeding upon the body and blood of the Lord, our 'youth is renewed like the eagle's' (*Psa.* 103:5).

iii. *Consider Christ's readiness to dispense divine blessings in this ordinance.* Jesus Christ is not a 'sealed fountain', but 'a flowing fountain'. We need but cry and he gives the breast. We need but thirst, and he opens the conduit. 'Let him that is athirst come, and whosoever will, let him take the water of life freely' (*Rev.* 22:17). As the clouds have a natural propensity to drop down their moisture upon the earth, so hath Christ to give forth of his gracious virtues and influences to the soul.

iv. *There is no danger of excess at this Supper.* Other feasts do often cause surfeit. It is not so here. The more we take of the bread of Life, the more healthy we are, and the more we come to our spiritual complexion. Fullness here doth not increase humours, but comforts; in spiritual things there is no extreme. Though a drop of Christ's blood be sweet, yet the more the better, the deeper the sweeter: 'Drink abundantly, O beloved' (*Song of Sol.* 5:1). In the original it is, 'Be ye inebriated with my love.'

v. *We know not how long this feast may last;* while the manna is to be had, let us bring our omer. God will not always be spreading the cloth. If people lose their stomach, he will call to the enemy to take it away.

vi. *Feeding upon Christ sacramentally will be a good preparative to sufferings.* The bread of life will help us to feed upon the bread of affliction. The 'cup of blessing' will enable us to drink of the cup of persecution. Christ's blood is a wine that hath a flavour in it, and is full of spirits. Therefore Cyprian tells us that, when the primitive Christians were to appear before the cruel tyrants, they were wont to receive the sacrament, and then they arose up from the Lord's table, as lions breathing forth the fire of heavenly courage (*tanquam leones ignem spiritus*)!

Let the following considerations also be as sauce to sharpen our appetite to the Lord's table. God loves to see us feed hungrily upon the bread of life.

5. *If we would come prepared to this ordinance, we must come with penitent hearts*, 'whose souls have been pierced, though not with a sword' (Augustine). The passover was to be eaten with 'bitter herbs'. We must bring our 'myrrh' of repentance which, though it be bitter to us, is sweet to Christ: 'They shall look upon me

whom they have pierced, and mourn over him' (*Zech.* 12:10). A broken Christ is to be received into a broken heart. We that have sinned with Peter should weep with Peter. Our eyes should be broached with tears, and our hearts steeped in the brinish waters of repentance. Say, 'Lord Jesus, though I cannot bring sweet spices, and perfume thy body as Mary did, yet I will wash thy feet with my tears.' The more bitterness we taste in sin, the more sweetness we shall taste in Christ.

6. *We must come with sincere hearts.* The tribes of Israel, being straitened in time, wanted some legal purifications; yet because their hearts were sincere, and they came with desire to meet with God in the passover, therefore the LORD healed the people (*2 Chron.* 30:19). Bad aims will spoil good actions. An archer may miss the mark as well by looking asquint as by shooting short. What is our design in coming to the sacrament? *Finis nobilitat opus* (the end makes known the work). Is it that we may have more victory over our corruptions, and be more confirmed in holiness? Then God will be good to us and heal us. Sincerity, like true gold, shall have some grains allowed for its lightness.

7. *We must come with hearts fired with love to Christ.* The spouse was in a burning fit of love, 'I am sick of love' (*Song of Sol.* 2:5). Let us give Christ the wine of our love to drink, and weep that we can love him no more. Would we have Christ's exhilarating presence in the Supper?

Let us meet him with strong endearments of affection. Basil[1] compares love to sweet ointment: Christ delights to smell this perfume. The disciple that did love most, Christ took him in his bosom. *Habitus sine exercitio similis est taciturnae lyrae* [A disposition not put into practice is like a silent lyre].

---

[1] Basil the Great (329–79), one of the Cappadocian Fathers. He vehemently opposed Arianism while Bishop of Caesarea.

8

True and False Faith

*But let a man examine himself, and so let him
eat of that bread, and drink of that cup*
(1 Cor. 11:28).

L et us exercise *the eye of faith*. Faith hath an eagle's
eye: it pierceth into things far remote from sense, it
sees the deep things of God. Look up unto Jesus, who was
lifted up upon the cross. If the brazen serpent had not
been looked upon, there had been no virtue in it; it would
not cure a blind Israelite: so though Christ was lifted up
upon the pole of the cross, yet he will not save those that
do not look up to him. Look upon Christ with a believing
eye, and you shall one day see him with a glorified eye.

Let us exercise also *the mouth of faith*. '*Quid par est
dentem et ventrem? Crede et manducasti*' [What is

appropriate for mouth and belly? Believing and eating] (Augustine). Here is the bread broken. Adam *died* by eating; we *live* by eating. In the sacrament, the whole of Christ is served up to us, the divine and human natures. All kinds of virtues come from him: mortifying, mollifying, comforting. Oh, then feed on him. This grace of faith is the great grace to be set to work at the sacrament.

QUESTION: But does the virtue lie simply in faith?

ANSWER: Not in faith considered purely as a grace, but as it has respect to the object. The virtue is not in faith, but in Christ. A ring which has a precious stone in it which will stanch blood, we say the ring stanches blood; but the virtue does not lie barely in the ring, but in the stone in the ring. So faith is the ring, Christ is the precious stone; all that faith does is to bring home Christ's merits to the soul, and so it justifies; the virtue is not in faith, but in Christ.

QUESTION: But why should faith carry away more from Christ in the sacrament than any other grace?

ANSWER: 1. Because faith is the most receptive grace; it is the receiving of enriching gold. So faith receiving of Christ's merit, and filling the soul with all the fullness of God, it must needs be an enriching grace. In the body there are veins that suck the nourishment which comes into the stomach; faith is such a sucking vein that draws virtue from Christ, therefore it is called a 'precious faith' (*2 Pet.* 1:1).

2. Faith has more of Christ's benefits annexed to it because it is the most humble grace. If repentance should fetch justification from Christ, a man would be ready to say, 'This was for my tears.' But faith is humble, it is an empty hand, and what merit can be in that? Does a poor man reaching out his hand merit an alms?

If we would come rightly prepared to the sacrament we must come with humble hearts. We see Christ humbling himself to the death; and will a humble Christ ever be received into a proud heart? 'He honoured the Father, not that thou shouldest dishonour him, but rather admire him, and learn from the act that he is a true Son in honouring his Father more than all besides' (Chrysostom).

A sight of God's glory, and a sight of sin, may humble us. Was Christ humble, who was all purity? And are we proud, who are all leprosy? Oh, let us come with a sense of our own vileness. How humble should he be who is to receive an alms of free grace!

Jesus Christ is a 'lily of the valleys' (*Song of Sol.* 2:1), not of the mountains. Humility was never a loser. The emptier the vessel is, and the lower it is let down into the well, the more water it draws up; so the more the soul is emptied of itself, and the lower it is let down by humility, the more it fetches out of the well of salvation. God will come into a humble heart to revive it (*Isa.* 57:15). That is no part of Christ's temple which is not built with a low roof.

We must come with heavenly hearts. The mystery of the sacrament is heavenly, what should an earthworm do here? He is not fit to feed on Christ's body and blood who, with the serpent, eats dust. The sacrament is called *koinonia*, a 'communion' (*1 Cor.* 10:16). What communion can an earthly man have with Christ? First, there must be conformity, before communion: he that is earthly is no more conformed in likeness to Christ than a clod of dust is to a star. An earthly man makes the world his god. Then let him not think to receive another God in the sacrament. Oh, let us be in the heavenly altitudes, and by the wing of grace ascend.

We must come with believing hearts. Christ gave the sacrament to the Apostles principally as they were believers. Such as come faithless, go away fruitless. Nor is it enough to have the habit of faith, but we must exert and put forth the vigorous actings of faith in this ordinance.

So that, because faith is humble, and gives all the glory to Christ, and free grace, hence it is God that has put so much honour upon it; this shall be the grace to which Christ and all his merits belong.

Therefore, above all graces, set faith to work in the sacrament. 'By faith we suck the blood of Christ, and thrust our tongue into the wounds of our Redeemer' (Cyrpian).[1] Faith fetches in all provisions. This is the

[1] *Per fidem Christi sanguinem sugimus et inter redemptoris nostri vulnera linguam figimus.*

golden bucket that draws water out of the well of life.

But there is a bastard faith in the world. Pliny[1] tells of a Cyprian stone which is in colour and splendour like the diamond, but it is not of the right kind, it will break with the hammer. So there is a false faith which sparkles and makes a show in the eye of the world, but it is not genuine, it will break with the hammer of persecution. Therefore, to prevent mistakes, that we may not be deceived and think we believe when we presume, I shall give you six differences between a sincere faith, which is the flower of the Spirit, and a hypocritical faith, which is the fruit of fancy.

1. *A hypocritical faith is easily come by.*

It is like the seed in the parable, which sprang up 'suddenly' (*Mark* 4:5). A false faith shoots up without any convictions and soul-humblings. As Isaac asked, 'How is it that thou hast found it [the venison] so quickly, my son?' (*Gen.* 27:20); so how comes this man by his faith so soon? Surely it is of a nature different from the true, and will quickly wither away. '*Solent praecocia subito flaccescere*' [Things which ripen prematurely usually wither suddenly]. But true faith, being an outlandish [foreign] plant, and of a heavenly extract, is hardly come by; it costs many a sigh and tear (*Acts* 2:37). This spiritual infant is not born without pangs.

---

[1] Pliny the Elder (23–79 AD), the author of a vast *Natural History*. He died observing the eruption of Mount Vesuvius in 79 AD.

2. *A hypocritical faith is afraid to come to trial.*

The hypocrite would rather have his faith commended than examined. He can no more endure a Scripture-trial, than counterfeit metal can endure the touchstone.

He is like a man that has stolen goods in his house and is very unwilling to have his house searched. So the hypocrite has forgotten some stolen goods that the devil has helped him to, and he is loth to have his heart searched. Whereas true faith is willing to come to a trial: 'Examine me, O LORD, and prove me; try my reins and my heart' (*Psa.* 26:2). David was not afraid to be tried by a jury; no, though God himself were one of the jury. Good wares are never afraid of the light.

3. *A hypocritical faith has a slight esteem of true faith.*

The hypocrite hears others speak in the commendation of faith, but he wonders where the virtue of it lies. He looks upon faith as a drug or some base commodity that will not sell; he will part with all the faith he has for a piece of silver, and perhaps it might be dear enough at the price. But that man who has true faith, he sets a high value upon it; he reckons this grace among the jewels. '*Plus fulget fides quam aurum*' [Faith shines more than gold] (Augustine).

What incorporates him into Christ, but faith? What puts him into a state of sonship, but faith? (*Gal.* 3:26). Oh, precious faith! A believer would not exchange his 'shield of faith' for a crown of gold.

4. *A hypocritical faith has a disability in one hand.*

With one hand it would take Christ, but it does not, with the other hand, give up itself to Christ. It would take Christ for the sake of security, but not give up itself to him by way of surrender. However, '*subiata quicunque parte integrante tollitur totum*' [If you take away any essential part, you take away the whole]. Whereas true faith is impartial – it takes Christ as a Saviour, and submits to him as a Prince. Christ says, 'With my body and my blood I thee endow', and faith says, 'With my soul I thee worship.'

5. *A hypocritical faith is impure.*

The hypocrite says he believes, yet he goes on in sin. He is all creed, but no commandments. He believes, yet will take God's name in vain: 'Wilt not thou from this time cry unto me, My father, thou art the guide of my youth? . . . Behold, thou hast spoken and done evil things as thou couldest' (*Jer.* 3:4–5).

These impostors would call God their Father, yet sinned as fast as they could. For one to say he has faith, yet to live in sin, is as if a man should say he were in health, yet his vitals are perished. But a true faith is joined with sanctity: 'Holding the mystery of the faith in a pure conscience' (*1 Tim.* 3:9). The jewel of faith is always put in the cabinet of a good conscience. The woman that touched Christ by faith felt a healing virtue coming from him. Though faith does not wholly remove sin, yet it subdues it.

6. *A hypocritical faith is a dead faith*, it tastes no sap, or sweetness in Christ. The hypocrite tastes something in the vine and olive, he finds contentment in the carnal luscious delights of the world, but no sweetness in a promise; the Holy Ghost himself is spiritless to him.

That is a dead faith which has no sense of taste. But true faith finds much delectation in heavenly things. The Word is sweeter than the honeycomb (*Psa.* 19:10). Christ's love is better than wine (*Song of Sol.* 1:2). Thus we see a difference between the true faith and the spurious. How many have thought they have had the live child of faith by them, when it has proved the dead child.

Take heed of presumption, but cherish faith. Faith applies Christ, and makes a spiritual concoction of his body and blood. 'Thou comest to Christ, not by the flesh but with the heart; I learn Christ, not with the mouth, but by faith' (Augustine).[1] This Supper was intended chiefly for believers (*Luke* 22:19). Christ's blood to an unbeliever is like aqua vitae in a dead man's mouth: it loses all its virtue.

We must come to the Lord's table with charitable hearts. 'Purge out therefore the old leaven . . . the leaven of malice and wickedness' (*1 Cor.* 5:7–8). The leaven of malice will sour the ordinance to us. Though we must come with bitter tears, yet not with bitter spirits. The

---

[1] *Accedis ad Christum non carne sed corde, edisco Christum non dente sed fide.*

Lord's Supper is 'agape': a love-feast (Ignatius). Christ's blood was shed to reconcile us, not only to God, but one to another. Christ's body was broken to make up the breaches among Christians. How sad it is that they who profess they are going to eat Christ's flesh in the sacrament should tear the flesh one of another! 'Whosoever hateth his brother, is a murderer' (*1 John* 3:15). He who comes to the Lord's table in hatred is a Judas to Christ, and a Cain to his brother. What benefit can he receive at the sacrament, whose heart is envenomed with malice?

If one drinks down poison, and presently takes a cordial, surely the cordial will do him no good. Such as are poisoned with rancour and malice are not the better for the sacrament cordial. He that does not come in charity to the sacrament has nothing of God in him, for 'God is love' (*1 John* 4:8).

He knows nothing of the gospel savingly, for it is a 'gospel of peace' (*Eph.* 6:15). He has none of the wisdom which comes from heaven, for that is 'gentle' and 'easy to be intreated' (*James* 3:17).

Oh, that Christians were, as Ignatius speaks, 'rooted and cemented together in love'! Shall devils unite, and saints divide? Did we thus learn Christ? Has not the Lord Jesus loved us to the death? What greater reproach can be cast upon such a loving Head than for the members to smite one against another? The good Lord put out the fire of contention and kindle the fire of love and amity in all our hearts!

We must come hither with praying hearts. Every ordinance, as well as every creature, is 'sanctified by . . . prayer' (*1 Tim*. 4:5). '*Oratio mutat elementum in alimentum*' [Prayer turns the element into spiritual aliment, or nourishment]. When we send the dove of prayer to heaven, it brings an olive leaf in its mouth.

We should pray that God would enrich his ordinance with his presence; that he would make the sacrament effectual to all those holy ends and purposes for which he hath appointed it; that it may be the feast of our graces, and the funeral of our corruptions; that it may not only be a sign to represent, but an instrument to convey, Christ to us, and a seal to assure us of our heavenly jointure [union]. If we would have the fat and sweet of this ordinance, we must send prayer before, as a harbinger, to bespeak a blessing.

Many seem so distracted with worldly cares that they can scarce spare any time for prayer before they come to the sacrament. Do they think the tree of blessing will drop its fruit into their mouth when they never shook it by prayer? God does not set his mysteries at so low a rate as to cast them away upon those that do not seek them (*Ezek*. 36:37).

Nor is it enough to pray, but it must be with heat and intenseness of soul. Jacob wrestled in prayer (*Gen*. 32:24). Cold prayers, like cold suitors, never speed. Prayer must be with sighs and groans (*Rom*. 8:26). It must be 'in the Holy Ghost' (*Jude* 20). He who will speak to God, says Ambrose, must speak to him in his own language which he understands, that is, in the language of his Spirit.

And lastly, *we must come to the Lord's table with self-denying hearts*. When we have prepared ourselves in the best manner we can, let us take heed of trusting to our preparations. 'So likewise ye, when ye shall have done all those things which are commanded you, say, We are unprofitable servants: we have done that which was our duty to do' (*Luke* 17:10). Use duty, but do not idolize it. We ought to use duties to fit us for Christ, but we must not make a Christ of our duties. Duty is the golden path to walk in, but not a silver crutch to lean on.

Alas, what are all our preparations? God can spy a hole in our best garments. 'Woe to man, if thou shouldst examine him and weigh him up' (Augustine).[1] 'All our righteousnesses are as filthy rags' (*Isa.* 64:6).

When we have prepared ourselves, as hoping in God's mercy, we must deny ourselves, as deserving his justice. If our holiest services be not sprinkled with Christ's blood, they are no better than shining sins, and, like Uriah's letter, they carry in them the matter of our death. Use duty, but trust to Christ and free grace for acceptance. Be like Noah's dove: she made use of her wings to fly, but trusted to the ark for safety.

We see how we are to be qualified in our approaches to the Lord's table. Thus coming, we shall meet with

---

[1] *Vae homini si eum trutina discutias*, etc.

embraces of mercy. We shall have not only a representation, but a participation, of Christ in the sacrament; we shall carry away not only *panis* [bread] but *salutaris* [healing]; we shall be 'filled with all the fulness of God' (*Eph.* 3:19).

9

Objections against Coming to the Sacrament

And when the people were come into the wood, behold,
the honey dropped; but no man put his hand to his
mouth: for the people feared the oath
(1 Sam. 14:26).

Has Jesus Christ made his gospel-banquet? Is he both the founder and the feast? Then let poor doubting Christians be encouraged to come to the Lord's table. Satan would hinder from the sacrament, as Saul did the people from eating honey (*1 Sam*. 14:26). But is there any soul that has been humbled and bruised for sin, whose heart secretly pants after Christ, but yet stands trembling, and dares not approach to these holy mysteries? Let me encourage that soul to come: 'Arise, he calleth thee' (*Mark* 10:49).

OBJECTION 1: *But I am sinful and unworthy*, and why should I meddle with such holy things?

ANSWER: Who did Christ die for but such? 'Christ Jesus came into the world to save sinners' (*1 Tim.* 1:15). He took our sins upon him, as well as our nature. 'Surely he hath borne our griefs' (*Isa.* 53:4). In the Hebrew it is our *sicknesses*. See thy sins, says Luther, upon Christ, and then they are no more thine, but his.[1] Our sins should humble us, but they must not discourage us from Christ; the more diseased we are, the rather we should step into this Pool of Siloam.

Who does Christ invite to the supper, but the poor, halt, and maimed (*Luke* 14:21)? That is, such as see themselves unworthy, and fly to Christ for sanctuary. The priest was to take a bunch of hyssop and dip it in the blood and sprinkle it upon the leper (*Lev.* 14:7). Thou who hast the leprosy of sin upon thee, yet if as a leper thou dost loathe thyself, Christ's precious blood shall be sprinkled upon thee.

OBJECTION 2: *But I have sinned presumptuously against mercy*. I have contracted guilt after I have been at the Lord's table, and surely Christ's blood is not for me?

ANSWER: It is indeed grievous to abuse mercy: it was the aggravation of Solomon's sin; his heart was turned from the Lord, 'which had appeared unto him twice', (*1 Kings*

---

[1] *Aspice peccata tua humeris Christi imposita, tum dices, peccata mea, non sunt mea, sed aliena.*

11:9). Presumptuous sins open the mouth of conscience to accuse, and shut the mouth of God's Spirit which should speak peace. Yet cast not away your anchor, look up to the blood of Christ; it can forgive sins against mercy. Did not Noah sin against mercy, who, though he had been so miraculously preserved in the flood, yet soon after he came out of the ark, he was drunk?

Did not David sin against mercy when, after God had made him king, he stained his soul with lust, and his robe with blood? Yet both their sins were washed away in that fountain which is set open for Judah to wash in (*Zech.* 13:1).

Did not the disciples deal unkindly with Christ in the time of his suffering? Peter denied him, and all the rest fled from his colours, 'Then all the disciples forsook him and fled' (*Matt.* 26:56). Yet Christ did not take advantage of their weakness, nor did he cast them off, but sends the joyful news of his resurrection to them (*Matt.* 27:7). And of his ascension, 'Go to my brethren, and say unto them, I ascend to my Father, and your Father; and to my God, and your God' (*John* 20:17).

And lest Peter should think he was none of the number that should be interested in Christ's love, therefore Christ despatched a special message by the angel to Peter to comfort him: 'Go tell his disciples *and Peter* that he goeth before you into Galilee: there shall ye see him, as he said unto you' (*Mark* 16:7).

So that where our hearts are sincere, and our turnings aside are rather from a defect in our power than our will, the Lord Jesus will not take advantage of every failing, but will drop his blood upon us, which has a voice in it which 'speaketh better things than that of Abel' (*Heb.* 12:24).

OBJECTION 3: *But I find such a faintness and feebleness in my soul that I dare not go to the Lord's table.*

ANSWER: Thou hast the more need to go: drink of this 'wine for . . . thine often infirmities' (*1 Tim.* 5:23). Were it not strange for a man to argue thus, 'My body is weak and declining, therefore I will not go to the physician'? He should the rather go. Our weakness should send us to Christ; his blood is mortal to sin, and vital to grace.

Thou sayest thou hast defects in thy soul; if thou hadst none, there would be no need of a Mediator, nor would Christ have any work to do. Oh, therefore turn thy disputing into believing, be encouraged to come to this blessed Supper. Thou shalt find Christ giving forth his sweet influences, and thy grace shall flourish as an herb.

OBJECTION 4: *But I have often come to this ordinance, and find no fruit, I am not filled with comfort.*

RESPONSE: God may meet thee in an ordinance, when thou dost not discern it. Christ was with Mary, yet she did not know it was Christ. Thou thinkest Christ hath not met thee at his table, because he doth not give thee comfort.

i. Though he doth not fill thee with comfort, he may fill thee with strength. We think we have no answer from God in duty, unless he fills us with joy. But God may manifest his presence as well by strength as by comfort. If we have power from heaven to foil our corruptions, and to walk more closely and evenly with God, this is an answer from God. 'I will strengthen them in the LORD; and they shall walk up and down in his name, saith the LORD' (*Zech.* 10:12). If, Christian, thou hast not God's arm to embrace thee, yet if thou hast his arm to strengthen thee, this is the fruit of an ordinance.

ii. If God does not fill thy heart with joy, yet if he fills thy eyes with tears, this is his meeting thee at his table. When thou lookest upon Christ broken on the cross, and considerest his love, and thy ingratitude, this makes the dew begin to fall, and thy eyes are like the 'fishpools in Heshbon' (*Song of Sol.* 7:4), full of water. This is God's gracious meeting thee in the sacrament. Bless his name for it. It is a sign, and the Sun of righteousness has risen upon us, when our frozen hearts melt in tears for sin.

iii. If thy comforts are low, yet if the actings of thy faith be high, this is God's manifesting his presence in the Supper. The sensible tokens of God's love are withheld, but the soul ventures on Christ's blood; it believes that coming to him, he will hold out the golden sceptre (*John* 6:37). This glorious acting of faith, and the inward quiet that faith breeds, is the blessed return of an ordinance. 'He will turn again, he will have compassion upon us; he will subdue our iniquities' (*Mic.* 7:19). The church's comforts were darkened, but her faith breaks forth as the sun out of a cloud. 'He will have compassion upon us.' This acting of faith makes us in a blessed condition; 'Blessed are they that have not seen, and yet have believed' (*John* 20:29).

OBJECTION 5: *But I cannot find any of these things in the sacrament, my heart is dead and locked up, and I have no return at all.*

ANSWER: Wait for God to give an answer of the ordinance. God has not promised to satiate the soul. '*Promissa Dei cadunt in debitum*' [The promises of God constitute an obligation upon him]. He 'filleth the hungry soul with goodness' (*Psa.* 107:9). If not with gladness, yet with goodness; the soul must be filled, or how can the promise be fulfilled?

Christian, God has said it, therefore wait. Wilt not thou believe God, unless thou hast a voice from heaven? The Lord hath given thee his promise; and is it not as good security to have a bill under a man's hand as to have it by word of mouth? Be content to wait awhile, mercy will come. God's mercies in Scripture, are not called *speedy* mercies, but they are '*sure* mercies' (*Isa.* 55:3).

Has Christ given us his body and blood? Then when we are at this gospel-ordinance, let us remember the Lord

Jesus there. The sacrament is a Christ-remembering ordinance, 'This do ye . . . in remembrance of me' (*1 Cor.* 11:25). God has appointed this spiritual festival, to preserve the living memory of our dying Saviour. A sacrament day is a commemoration day.

1. *Remember Christ's passion.* '*Memoriam passionis meae animis vestris recolite*' [Bring back to your minds the memory of my passion]. 'Remembering mine affliction and my misery, the wormwood and the gall' (*Lam.* 3:19). I may alter the words a little, 'Remembering the vinegar and the gall.' If the manna was to be kept in the ark, that the memory of it should be preserved, how should the death and suffering of Christ be kept in our minds as a memorial, when we are at the table of the Lord?

2. *Remember the glorious benefits we receive from the broken body of Christ.* We usually remember those things which are advantageous to us.

Christ's broken body is a screen to keep off the fire of God's wrath from us. Christ's body being broken, the serpent's head is broken. Christ being broken upon the cross, a box of precious jewels is broken open: now we have access to God with boldness.

The blood of the cross has made way to the throne of grace. Now we are made sons and heirs; and to be heir to the promise is better than to be heir to the crown. Christ having died, we are made near kin to the blessed Trinity;

we are candidates and expectants of glory. The bloody way of the cross, is our *via lactea*, our milky way to heaven. Jesus Christ drank gall that we might drink the honey streams of Canaan. His cross was stuck full of nails, that our crown might be hung full of jewels. Well may we remember Christ in the blessed sacrament.

But it is not the bare remembrance of Christ's death that is enough. Some who have a natural tenderness of spirit may be affected by the history of Christ's passion; but this remembrance of Christ has little comfort in it. Let us remember Christ in the sacrament aright:

i. *Let us remember Christ's death with joy.* 'God forbid that I should glory, save in the cross of our Lord Jesus Christ' (*Gal.* 6:14). When we see Christ in the sacrament, crucified before our eyes, we may behold him in that posture as he was in upon the cross, stretching out his blessed arms to receive us. Oh, what matter of triumph and acclamation is this! Though we remember our sins with grief, yet we should remember Christ's sufferings with joy. Let us weep for those sins which shed his blood, yet rejoice in that blood which washes away our sins.

ii. *Let us so remember Christ's death, as to conform to his death.* 'Being made conformable unto his death' (*Phil.* 3:10). Then we remember Christ's death aright, when we are dead with him; our pride and passion are dead. Christ's dying for us makes sin die in us; then we rightly remember Christ's crucifixion, when we are crucified with him, when we are dead to the pleasures and preferments of the world. 'The world is crucified unto me, and I unto the world' (*Gal.* 6:14).

If Jesus Christ has given us this soul-festival for the strengthening of grace, let us labour to feel some virtue flowing out of this ordinance to us.

Let not the sacrament be a dry breast. It were strange if a man should receive no nourishment from his food. It is a discredit to this ordinance if we get no increase of grace. Shall leanness enter into our souls at a 'feast of fat things'? Christ gives us his body and blood for the augmenting of faith; he expects that we should reap some profit and income, and that our weak, minute faith should flourish into a great faith, 'O woman, great is thy faith' (*Matt.* 15:28)! It were good to examine whether, after our frequent celebration of his holy Supper, we have arrived at a 'great faith'.

QUESTION: How may I know whether I have this great faith?

ANSWER For the solution of this, I shall lay down six eminent signs of a 'great faith'; and if we can show any one of them, we have made a good proficiency in the sacrament.

1. *A great faith can trust God without a pawn, or security*; it can rely upon providence in the deficiency of

outward supplies. 'Although the fig tree shall not blossom, neither shall fruit be in the vines; the labour of the olive shall fail, and the fields shall yield no meat . . . yet I will rejoice in the LORD' (*Hab.* 3:17–18).

An unbeliever must have something to feed his senses, or he gives up the ghost. When he is at his wealth's end, he is at his wits' end. Faith does not question that God will provide, though it sees not which way provisions should come in. '*Fides famem non formidat*' [Faith does not fear famine]. God has set his seal to it, 'Verily, thou shalt be fed' (*Psa.* 37:3). Faith puts the bond in suit, 'Lord', says faith, 'wilt thou feed the birds of the air, and wilt thou not feed me? Shall I want when my Father keeps the purse?'

A good Christian, with the rod of faith, smites the rock of heaven, and some honey and oil comes out for the supply of his present necessities.

2. *A great faith is a wonder-working faith.* It can do those things which exceed the power of nature. A great faith can open heaven, it can overcome the world (*1 John* 5:4); it can master a tendency to sin (*2 Sam.* 22:24); it can prefer the glory of God before secular interest (*Rom.* 9:1); it can rejoice in affliction (*1 Thess.* 1:6).

It can bridle the intemperancy of passion; it can shine forth in the hemisphere of its relations; it can do duties in a more refined and sublimated manner, mixing love with duty, which mellows it, and makes it taste more pleasant. It can anticipate glory. '*Fides attingit inaccessa, prospicit novissima'* [Faith reaches what cannot be approached and looks forward to the last things]. It makes things at the greatest distance to unite. Thus the springhead of faith rises higher than nature. A man by the power of nature can no more do this than iron can of itself swim or the earth ascend.

3. *A great faith is firm and steadfast;* weak faith is frequently shaken with fear and doubts. A great faith is like an oak that spreads its roots deep and is not easily blown down (*Col.* 2:7). A great faith is like the anchor or cable of a ship that holds it steady in the midst of storms. A Christian who is steeled with this heroic faith is settled in the mysteries of religion. The Spirit of God has so firmly printed heavenly truths upon his heart that you may as well remove the sun out of the firmament as remove him from those holy principles he has absorbed. Behold here, a pillar in the temple of God (*Rev.* 3:12).

4. *A great faith can trust in an angry God;* it believes God's love through a frown (*Jon.* 2:4). A vigorous faith, though it be repulsed and beaten back, yet it will come on again, and press upon God with a holy obstinacy. The woman of Canaan was three times repulsed by Christ, yet she would take no denial from him; she turned discouragements into arguments, and made a fresh onset upon Christ, till at last by the power of faith, she overcame him, 'O woman, great is thy faith: be it unto thee even as thou wilt' (*Matt.* 15:28). The key of her faith

unlocked Christ's bowels, and now she may have what she will from him. When once she had gotten his heart, she might have his treasure too.

5. *A great faith can swim against the tide*; it can go across both sense and reason. Corrupt reason says, as Peter, 'Pity thyself, Lord' (*Matt.* 16:22 [margin]); faith says, It is better to suffer than sin. Reason consults safety; faith will hazard safety to preserve sanctity. A believer can sail to heaven, though the tide of reason and the wind of temptation be against him.

Abraham in the case of sacrificing his son, did not call reason to the council-board. When God said, 'Offer up thy son Isaac', it was enough to perplex not only fleshly wisdom, but even faith too. For here the commands of God did seem to interfere. In one command the Lord said, 'Thou shalt not murder', and behold here is a quite contrary command, 'Offer up thy son.' So that Abraham, in obeying one command, seemed to disobey another.

Besides, Isaac was a son of the promise; the Messiah was to come from Isaac's line (*Heb.* 11:18). And if he be cut off, where shall the world have a Mediator? Here was enough to trouble and puzzle this holy patriarch yet Abraham's faith unties all these knots, and the bloody knife is made ready.

Abraham believed that when God called for it, it was not murder, but sacrifice; and that the Lord having made a promise of Christ's springing out of Isaac's loins, rather than that the promise should fall to the ground, God could raise up seed out of Isaac's ashes. Here was a giant faith, which God himself did set a trophy of honour upon, 'By myself I have sworn, saith the LORD, for because thou hast done this thing, and hast not withheld thy son, thine only son: that in blessing I will bless thee' (*Gen.* 22:16).

6. *A great faith can bear great delays.* Though God does not give a present answer to prayer, faith believes it shall have an answer in due time. A weak faith is soon out of breath, and if it has not the mercy presently, it begins to faint; whereas he who has a strong vibrant faith 'shall not make haste' (*Isa.* 28:16). A great faith is content to stay at God's leisure. Faith will trade with God for time. 'Lord', says faith, 'if I have not the mercy I want instantly, I will trust longer; I know my money is in good hands; an answer of peace will come. Perhaps the mercy is not yet ripe, or perhaps I am not yet ripe for the mercy. Lord, do as it seems good in thine eyes.'

Faith knows that the most tedious voyages have the richest returns; and the longer mercy is in expectation, the sweeter it will be in fruition, '*Quo longius defertur cor suavius laetatur*' [The more the heart is kept waiting, the more sweetly it rejoices].

Behold here a glorious faith; if we have such a faith as this to show, it is blessed fruit of our sacramental converse with God. But I would not discourage infant-believers. If your grace be not risen to the size and proportion of a great faith, yet if it be of a proper kind, it shall find acceptance. God who bids us to receive him who is 'weak in the faith' (*Rom.* 14:1) will not himself refuse him. If your faith be not grown to a cedar, yet if it be a 'bruised reed', it is too good to be broken (*Matt.* 12:20). A weak faith can lay hold on a strong Christ. A palsied hand may tie the knot in marriage.

Only, let not Christians rest in lower measures of grace, but aspire after higher degrees. The stronger our faith, the firmer is our union with Christ, and the more sweet influence we draw from him.

This is that which honours the blessed sacrament, when we can show an increase of grace; and, being strong in faith, bring glory to God (*Rom.* 4:20).

10

Thankfulness to God

I will offer to thee the sacrifice of thanksgiving,
and will call upon the name of the LORD
(Psa. 116:17).

Has Jesus Christ provided such a blessed banquet for us? Is it true that he does not nurse us abroad, but feeds us with his own breast, nay, his own blood? Let us then study to answer the great love of Christ.

It is true, we can never parallel his love; yet let us show ourselves thankful. We can do nothing *satisfactory*, but we may do something *gratulatory*. Christ gave himself a sin-offering for us, let us give ourselves a thank-offering to him. If a man redeem another out of debt, will he not be grateful? How deeply do we stand obliged to Christ, who had redeemed us from hell!

'When I shall have given him whatever I am, whatever I can, is it not as a spark to the sun, a drop to the river, a grain to the heap? I have nothing but two mites, body and soul' (Bernard).[1] And let us show our thankfulness in four ways.

1. *Let us show our thankfulness to Christ by courage.*

Christ has set us an example; he did not fear man, but 'endured the cross', and 'despised the shame'. Let us be steeled with courage, being ready to suffer for Christ, which is, as Chrysostom says, to be baptized with a baptism of blood. Did Christ bear the wrath of God for us, and shall not we bear the wrath of men for him? It is our glory to suffer in Christ's quarrel. 'If ye be reproached for the name of Christ, happy are ye; for the spirit of glory and of God resteth upon you' (*1 Pet.* 4:14). 'It is not possible that a man pursuing the course of virtue should not be exposed to grief, tribulation, and temptations, for how can he escape it, who is treading in the strait and narrow way?' (Chrysostom).

Let us pray for furnace-grace, to be like those three children, 'Be it known unto thee, O king, that we will not serve thy gods' (*Dan.* 3:18). They would rather burn than bow. Oh, that such a spirit as was in Cyprian might survive in us! When the Proconsul Galerius would have

---

[1] *Cum ei donavero quicquid sum, quicquid possum, non est tanquam scintilla ad solem, gutta ad fluvium, granum ad acervum? Non habeo nisi minuta duo, corpus et animam.* [An allusion to the story of the widow's mites (*Mark* 12:41–44; *Luke* 21:1–4).]

tempted him from religion, and said to him, '*Consule tibi*' [Consult for thy safety], he replied, 'In so just a cause, there is no need of consultation.' When the sentence of death was read, Cyprian replied, '*Deo gratias*', 'Thanks be to God!' We know not how soon an hour of temptation may come. Oh, remember, Christ's body was broken, his blood poured out; we have no such blood to shed for him, as he shed for us.

2. *Let us show our thankfulness to Christ by fruitfulness.*

Let us not be a dry tree, but by the grace of Christ, send forth a fruitful bough (Ambrose).[1] Let us bring forth the sweet fruits of patience, heavenly mindedness and good works. This is to live, not to ourselves, but to him who died for us, and rose again (*2 Cor.* 5:15). If we would rejoice the heart of Christ, and make him not repent of his sufferings, let us be fertile in obedience. The wise men did not only worship Christ, but presented unto him gifts, 'gold, and frankincense, and myrrh' (*Matt.* 2:11).

Let us present Christ with the best fruits of our garden; let us give him our love, that flower of delight. The saints are not only compared to stars for their knowledge, but spice-trees for their fertileness. Christ delighted in the breasts of his spouse because they were like 'clusters of grapes' (*Song of Sol.* 7:7). The blood of Christ, received in a spiritual manner, is like the 'water of jealousy', which

---

[1] *Lignum aridum factus, sed per gratiam Christi pomifera arbor pullulasti.*

had the virtue both to kill and to make fruitful (*Num.* 5:27–28). Christ's blood kills sin, and makes the heart fructify in grace.

3. *Let us show our thankfulness to Christ by zeal.*

How jealous was Christ for our redemption! Zeal turns a saint into a seraph. A true Christian has a double baptism, of water and fire. He is baptized with the fire of zeal. '*Zelus est gradus intensus purae affectionis*' [Zeal is an intense degree of pure affection]. Be zealous for Christ's Name and worship. Zeal is increased by opposition; it cuts its way through the rocks. Zeal loves truth most when it is disgraced and hated. 'They have made void thy law. Therefore I love thy commandments above gold' (*Psa.* 119:126–127).

How little thankfulness do they show to Christ who have no zeal for his honour and interest! They are like Ephraim, 'Ephraim is a cake not turned' (*Hos.* 7:8): Baked on one side, and dough on the other. Christ does most abominate a lukewarm temper (*Rev.* 3:15). He is even sick of such professors.

They who write of the situation of England say that it is seated between the torrid and frigid zones; the climate is neither very hot nor very cold. I wish this were not the temper of the people, and that our hearts were not too like the climate we live in. The Lord cause the fire of holy zeal to be always burning upon the altar of our hearts!

---

[1] *Zelus est gradus intensus purae affectionis.*

4. *Let us show our thankfulness by universal subjection to Christ.*

This is to make the Lord's Supper, in a spiritual sense, a feast of dedication, when we renew our vows, and give ourselves to God's service. 'Truly I am thy servant; I am thy servant, and the son of thy handmaid' (*Psa.* 116:16). Lord, all I have is thine. My head shall be thine to study for thee; my hands shall be thine to work for thee; my heart shall be thine to adore thee; my tongue shall be thine to praise thee!

11

Comforts for Believers, and Warnings to Unbelievers

Unto you therefore which believe he is precious:
but unto them which be disobedient . . . a
stone of stumbling and rock of offence
(1 Pet. 2:7–8).

If Jesus Christ has provided so holy an ordinance as the sacrament, let us walk suitably to it. Have we received Christ into our hearts? Let us show him forth by our heavenliness.

1. *Let us show forth Christ by our heavenly words.*

Let us speak 'the language of Canaan'. When the Holy Ghost came upon the apostles they spake with other tongues (*Acts* 2:4). While we speak the words of grace and soberness, our lips smell as perfume, and drop as honey.

2. *Let us show forth Christ by our heavenly affections.*
Let our sighs and breathings after God go up as a cloud
of incense: 'Set your affection on things above' (*Col.* 3:2).
We should do with our affections as the husbandmen do
with their corn; if the corn lie low in a damp room, it is
in danger to corrupt. Therefore, they carry it up into their
highest room, that it may keep better. So our affections, if
set upon the earth, are apt to corrupt and be unsavoury.
Therefore, we should carry them up on high, above the
world, that they may be preserved pure. Breathe after
fuller discoveries of God, desire to 'attain unto the resurrection of the dead' (*Phil.* 3:11). The higher our affections
are raised toward heaven, the sweeter joy we feel. The
higher the lark flies, the sweeter it sings.

3. *Let us show forth Christ, by our heavenly conver-
sation* (*Phil.* 3:20).

Hypocrites may, in a pang of conscience, have some
good affections stirred, but they are as flushings of heat in
the face, which come and go. But the constant tenor of
our life must be holy. We must shine forth in a kind of
angelical sanctity; as it is with a coin: it has not only the
sovereign's image within the ring; but his superscription
without. So it is not enough to have the image of Christ
in the heart, but there must be the superscription without;
something of Christ must be written in the life.

The scandalous lives of many communicants are a
reproach to the sacrament, and tempt others to atheism.
How odious it is that these hands which have received the

sacred elements should take bribes! That those eyes, which have been filled with tears at the Lord's table should afterwards be filled with envy! That those teeth, which have eaten holy bread should grind the faces of the poor! That those lips, which have touched the sacramental cup should salute a harlot! 'They have washed hands, but unwashed deeds' (Bernard).[1] That that mouth which has drunk consecrated wine should be full of oaths! That they who seem to deify Christ in the Eucharist should vilify him in his members! In a word, that such who pretend to eat Christ's body and drink his blood at church should 'eat the bread of wickedness, and drink the wine of violence', in their own houses (*Prov.* 4:17). These are like the Italians I have read of who, at the sacrament, are so devout, as if they believed God to be in the bread; but in their lives are so profane, as if they believed not God to be in heaven.

Such as these are apt to make the world think that the gospel is but a fancy, or religious cheat. What shall I say of them? They do, with Judas, receive the devil in the sop, and are no better than crucifiers of the Lord of glory. 'They tread the Lord under foot, and the blood they draw from the sweetest vine they pollute' (Bernard). As their sin is heinous, so their punishment will be proportional. 'He that eateth and drinketh unworthily, eateth and drinketh damnation to himself' (*1 Cor.* 11:29). If one of the vestal

[1] *Sunt lotis manibus, sed illotis operibus.*
[2] *Conculcant Dominum, et sanguinem dulcissimae vitis ducunt pollutum.*

virgins who had vowed herself to religion were deflowered, the Romans caused her to be buried alive, (Plutarch).[1] Such as have a sacramental vow upon them, yet afterwards deflower the virginity of their souls by scandalous sins, God will bury them alive in the flames of hell.

Oh, that such a lustre and majesty of holiness may sparkle forth in the lives of communicants that others may say, 'These have been with Jesus!', and that their consciences may lie under the power of this conviction, that the sacrament has a confirming and a transforming virtue in it!

A further use of the institution of the sacrament is of *comfort to God's people.*

1. *From Christ's body broken, and his blood poured out, we may gather this comfort: that it was a glorious sacrifice.*

i. *It was a sacrifice of infinite merit.* Had it been only an angel that suffered, or had Christ been only a mere man – as some blasphemously dream: 'They drank in the Ebionite opinion concerning bare humanity' (Tertullian)[2] – then we might have despaired of salvation. But he suffered for us, who was God, as well as man.

---

[1] Plutarch of Chaeronea (46–120 AD). In Roman antiquity, a number of virgins devoted themselves to maintaining a flame in honour of the goddess Vesta. Their vows involved chastity.

[2] Tertullian (c.150–220), first of the Latin fathers. Watson cites from his work *Against Praxeas.*

Therefore, the apostle calls it expressly, '*Sanguis Dei*' the blood of God (*Acts* 20:28). It is man that sins; it is God that dies. This is a sovereign cordial to believers. Christ having poured out his blood, now God's justice is completely satisfied. God was infinitely more contented with Christ's sufferings at mount Calvary than if we had lain in hell, and undergone his wrath for ever. The blood of Christ has quenched the flame of divine fury. And now what should we fear? All our enemies are either reconciled, or subdued; God is a reconciled enemy, and sin is a subdued enemy.

'Who shall lay anything to the charge of God's elect? . . . It is Christ that died' (*Rom.* 8:33–34). It is reported that when Satan once appeared to Luther, and thought to frighten him, Luther showed him that scripture, 'I will put enmity between thee and the woman, and between thy seed and her seed, and it shall bruise thy head' (*Gen.* 3:15), whereupon Satan vanished. So when the devil shall accuse us, let us show him the cross of Christ. When he brings his pencil, and goes to draw our sins in all their colours, let us bring the sponge of Christ's blood, and that will wipe them out again. All bonds are cancelled; whatsoever the law has charged upon us is discharged. The debt book is crossed with the blood of the Lamb.

ii. *It was a sacrifice of eternal duration.* The benefit of it is perpetuated. 'He entered in once into the holy place, having obtained eternal redemption for us' (*Heb.* 9:12). 'The apostle means that the sacrifice of Christ is always valid for true and lasting peace.'[1] Therefore, Christ is said to be 'a priest for ever' (*Heb.* 5:6), because the virtue and comfort of his sacrifice abides for ever.

2. *Christ's blood being shed, believers may lay claim to all heavenly privileges.* Wills are ratified by the death of the testator. 'A testament is of force after men are dead' (*Heb.* 9:17). It is observable in the text, Christ calls his blood, 'The blood of the New Testament': *'Sanguis quo foedus solenniter sancitur'* [The blood by which the covenant is solemnly ratified] (Grotius).[2] Christ made a will or testament and gave rich legacies to the saints: pardon of sin, grace and glory. The Scriptures are the rolls wherein these legacies are registered. Christ's blood is the sealing of the will.

This blood being shed, Christians may put in for a title to these legacies; 'Lord, pardon my sin, Christ has died for my pardon. Give me grace, Christ has purchased it by his blood.' The Testator having died, the will is in force. Christian, art thou not filled with joy? Art not thou possessed of heaven? Yet thou hast this confirmed by a Will. A man that has a deed sealed, making over such lands and tenements after the passing of a few years, though at present he has little to help himself with, yet he comforts himself when he looks upon his sealed deed, with hopes of that which is to come. So though at present

[1] *Innuit apostolus, Christi sacrificium ad veram, semperque mansuram valuisse.*

[2] Hugo Grotius (1583–1645), Dutch jurist and theologian.

we enjoy not the privileges of consolation, and glorification, yet we may cheer our hearts with this, 'The deed is sealed', the Will and Testament are ratified by the blood-shedding of Christ.

3. *Is Christ's blood shed? Here is comfort against death.* A dying Saviour sweetens the pangs of death. Is thy Lord crucified? Be of good comfort, Christ by dying has overcome death. He has cut the lock of sin, where the strength of death lay. Christ has knocked out the teeth of this lion. He has pulled the thorn out of death, that it cannot prick a believer's conscience. 'O death, I will be thy plagues' (*Hos.* 13:14). Christ has disarmed death, and taken away all its deadly weapons; so that, though it may strike, it cannot sting a believer. Christ has drawn the poison out of death, nay, has made death friendly. 'Christ has blunted the sting of death and broken its power, and now there comes about the abolition of sin and the passage to a better life.'[1]

This 'pale horse' (*Rev.* 6:8) carries a child of God home to his Father's house. Faith gives a propriety to heaven, death gives a possession. What sweet comfort may we draw from the crucifixion of our Lord! His precious blood makes the pale face of death to be of a ruddy and beautiful complexion.

---

[1] *Mortis aculeum retudit Christus, et vim infregit, iamque fit peccati abolitio, et ad vitam meliorem transitio.*

The final use of the doctrine of the sacrament is of *warning to the unrepentant sinner.*

Here is a dark side of the cloud to all profane persons who live and die in sin. They have no part in the blood of Christ. Their condition will be worse than if Christ had not died! Christ who is a lodestone to draw the elect to heaven, will be a millstone to sink the wicked deeper into hell.

There is a crew of sinners who slight Christ's blood, and swear by it; let them know his blood will cry against them. They must feel the same wrath which Christ felt upon the cross; and because they cannot bear it at once, they must undergo it throughout eternity (*2 Thess.* 1:9). So inconceivably torturing will this be that the damned know not how to endure it, nor yet how to avoid it.

Sinners will not believe this till it be too late. The mole is blind all its life, yet, as Pliny says, it begins to see when it dies: 'In dying man begins to open the eyes which were closed while he lived.'[1] Wicked men, while they live, are blinded by the god of this world (*2 Cor.* 4:4). But when they are dying, the eye of their conscience will begin to be opened and they shall see the wrath of God, flaming before their eyes; which sight will be a sad Prologue to an eternal tragedy.

---

[1] *Oculos incipit aperire moriendo quos clausos habuit vivendo.*